G000122486

securicor
The People Business

SARAH UNDERWOOD

CPL

Copyright © Securicor plc 1997

First published 1997 by
CPL Books
Oxford Centre for Innovation
Mill Street
Oxford OX2 0JX
United Kingdom

CPL Books is an imprint of Capstone Publishing Limited

British Library Cataloguing in Publication Data
A CIP catalogue record for this book is available from
the British Library

ISBN 1-901814-00-9

Typeset in 10.5/14 pt Times by
Susan Bushell/Oxford Air Research
Printed and bound in Great Britain by
T.J. International Ltd, Padstow, Cornwall

This book is printed on acid-free paper

Contents

Vigilant and Valiant

"Valour is a gift. Those having it never know for sure whether they have it until the test comes. And those having it in one test never know for sure if they will have it when the next test comes"

— Carl Sandburg, 1954

Foreword

Welcome to Securicor, a diverse and dynamic group which has built on the strengths of its people and its fundamental commitment to honesty and integrity to become a global supplier of first-class business services. As chairman and managing director of the Group during an exciting period of its growth, it seems fitting for me to invite you to review the first six decades of our business in the pages of this book, which both commemorates and celebrates the achievements of all those who have served the company.

From the chairman to the cash-in-transit driver, Securicor's philosophy has always been one of working together for the common cause, a family approach which has been at the heart of the Group's success and created many lasting friendships over the years.

My first encounter with Securicor was in 1951, when I joined the law practice of Hextall, Erskine & Company. The embryonic security firm was one of partner Keith Erskine's clients. Those were heady days, but only a forerunner to the eventful years which would follow Keith's purchase of Securicor and his installation as managing director in 1960.

Keith's talents were unique. His initial vision of the potential in the worldwide industrial security business has since been realised, while his entrepreneurial spirit guided the company into new activities including parcels delivery and industrial cleaning services. To fund this wealth of ideas he was fortunate in having a brother with a financially successful hotel business.

From a company with a staff of 300 and an annual turnover of £500,000, Keith grew a stock market quoted empire of 18,000 UK

Peter Smith OBE
Chairman and Managing Director
1974–1985
Non-executive Chairman 1985–1995

and 12,000 overseas employees. At the time of his unexpected death in 1974, Securicor was turning over £40 million a year.

That was my inheritance and it was a pleasure to spend the latter years of my career at the helm of such a seaworthy ship, working with a fine crew of loyal men and women devoted to serving customers and upholding Securicor's unimpeachable reputation for dedication, integrity and honesty.

When I retired in March 1995, it was with great sadness but also many happy memories. To my successor, Sir Neil Macfarlane, I was able to hand over a worldwide enterprise showing consistently increasing profits, at £80.6 million on a turnover of over £800 million, as well as my confidence in the men who led the Group's four business divisions in the security, parcels distribution, communications and business services markets.

This book tells the story of the people who have made Securicor a successful enterprise. Without their innovation and dedication a small, and sometimes struggling, security firm may well have slipped into the annals of history. Instead, as you turn the pages of this book, a picture of a vibrant, multi-disciplined organisation will emerge, robust enough to challenge the rigours of today's business environment while also maintaining the innovative edge which will ensure continuing prosperity into the new millennium.

Peter Smith OBE

A new millennium, a New Securicor — there could be no better time to draw one era of the Group's development to a close and embark upon a new journey, carrying with us all the benefits of a 1996 share restructure that saw the dual London Stock Exchange presence acquired through historical accident replaced by a single public limited company.

In fact, this book reflects our history up to the date of the share restructure, June 1996. A special addendum details the many changes which have occurred during the subsequent 15 months.

While the course we have set for Securicor plc is certainly demanding, the excitement both within the Group and across the investment community is contagious. To borrow from the 1933 inaugural address of Franklin D Roosevelt: 'Let me assert my firm belief that the only thing we have to fear is fear itself.'

Sir Neil Macfarlane
Non-executive Chairman

Having first joined Securicor Security Services as an adviser and non-executive director in 1991, it was with great pleasure that I accepted the board's invitation to become non-executive chairman of Securicor Group following the retirement of Peter Smith in 1995. Like him, I put my faith in the people who are Securicor, the pride they take in their work and the atmosphere which they have generated of a large and happy extended family with a valuable part to play in the local community and society as a whole.

Already a commercial success and with a presence in over 30 nations around the globe, Securicor is poised to bring its name before an even larger audience as it works with growing numbers of governments to tackle a relentless upsurge in the need for crime prevention. It is my job to open some of the doors to these new business partners, a task made easier by the company's demonstrable track record and the commitment of staff throughout the security division.

In Europe, the greatest challenge falls to the distribution business as it builds on 20 years of commitment to offer truly pan-European services. Having started life as a UK data courier service, Securicor Distribution has expanded to offer a wide portfolio of services, from same-day and overnight parcels and document delivery in the UK, to European parcel and freight distribution, air and sea freight, container distribution, warehousing and contract distribution. Its European network, spanning 16 countries, holds great promise as continental business increases and the division maximises its presence.

So too in North America does Securicor stand on the brink of great achievements, this time with its communications businesses which are charting new territories and complementing our tremendously successful UK investment in Cellnet, certainly one of the deals of the century.

Securicor's presence in cities from Nairobi to Caracas, from Hong Kong to Kuwait and from Budapest to Paris is a great tribute to all those who have dedicated their careers to the Group. But there is plenty still to be done in the world markets to which Securicor has decided to devote its efforts. Steeped in a rich and varied history and with a diversity of services all operating under the respected Securicor name, the Group has much to play for and much with which to reward its shareholders and staff.

As a united public limited company, Securicor is well-prepared to enter a new era as one of the UK's top companies, but it will never forget its roots nor the people who have in the past and will in the future carry its success throughout the world so proudly upon their shoulders.

Sir Neil Macfarlane

THE
PHILOSOPHY

1

"History is philosophy teaching by examples"

– Dionysius of Halicarnassus,
Antiquities of Rome

*"A wise man shall make more opportunities
than he finds"*

– Francis Bacon,
Essay 52, Of Ceremonies and Respects

THE PHILOSOPHY

The reflections of Dionysius of Halicarnassus and Francis Bacon are equally at home within the confines of the Securicor Group: many lessons have been learnt during the company's development, but so too have new ideas been its making.

From Keith Erskine, the man who put Securicor on the map, to today's group chief executive, Roger Wiggs, the organisation has consistently pushed forward, sometimes taking a wrong turning, but always ready to pick up the trail and head for undiscovered land.

This quest for adventure, instilled in the company from its earliest days by Erskine, is evident in the organisation's nature. A leader rather than a follower, Securicor is unlike so many of its peers in climbing to the top of many mountains, where most prefer to reach the peak of only one.

From its foundation as a small residential security firm, Erskine led the company to become a leading industrial security provider, as well as a force to be reckoned with in the parcel distribution business. More recent group chief executives have moved down the evolution and devolution road, creating communications and business services operations, and giving all full responsibility for their actions.

While each brought his own business philosophy and personal ambition to the job of group chief executive, all bar one share a common experience in having trained and practised as a lawyer. Indeed, with the exception of Peter Towle, all worked at Hextall Erskine & Company, acting as solicitors for the Group, before being enticed into full-time employment. With knowledge of the company and the legal disciplines of analysis and decision-making, their contribution was key to the management of new businesses, but also enhanced the essence of loyalty and integrity which was embedded from the earliest days when Securicor recruited ex-servicemen and women to meet its contracts for guarding and cash services.

The selection process was rigorous, with applicants having to provide details of 20 years' continuous employment as well as personal references. They were also required to declare that they had never been convicted of a criminal offence and sign a statement to confirm the given information. Despite the growth of

■

"Securicor has a strong strategy and I feel it is entirely appropriate to have a wide base within the group and a balanced platform which can take the strain and support our businesses wherever they are in the world"

— Roger Wiggs

■

the Group and the variety of its inherent functions, staff selection remained and remains equally formal — a far cry from the hire and fire mentality which is so often prevalent in an uncertain economic climate and a measure of the value Securicor attaches to the people who are its everyday interface with customers and the public alike.

Keen management interest in both business and personnel matters, albeit sometimes overpowering in the years of Keith Erskine, has proved a source of much success and provided the stability necessary to underpin such a disparate group. While Erskine had his own style of management, often offering both carrot and stick, the interest of management in all who work for Securicor and its businesses is a recurrent theme throughout the company's history.

Today, Roger Wiggs bears out the policy with a renewed focus on specific business lines and individuals. Rather than calling divisional chief executives together on a regular basis, Wiggs devised the Chief Executive's Review, which concentrates on each unit separately and brings more managers into divisional decision making, raising their profile and giving them a clearer view of the business.

To this vertical reporting process he has added breadth, allocating to each subsidiary board two non-executive members from elsewhere in the Group, furthering the transfer of skills and experience. Looking at the whole, it is a reimposition of the lasting philosophy of the importance of people within Securicor and a recognition of the need for a strong succession chain, the lack of which threatened to weaken the business in the latter years of Erskine's chairmanship.

Roger Wiggs' proposal aims to develop board members who will take the Group beyond the year 2000, a personal endorsement of Securicor's acknowledgement that staff are its most valuable asset and must be considered in every business decision.

Having created clear-cut career paths through divisionalisation and made changes to the reporting structure, the need for staff development is paramount, underlining the devotion to training which has passed down the generations of Securicor executives

Roger Wiggs

"I am always striving to do better and learning constantly as I go along"

Group Chief Executive Roger Wiggs has had a long and varied career with Securicor, giving him the business knowledge and management experience not only to make today's decisions but also to plan for tomorrow.

Joining the law practice of Hextall Erskine & Company when he was 16 years old, Wiggs aspired to becoming an articled clerk. After a year of making tea and running errands he was rewarded in January 1957 when he was articled to Peter Smith, then a partner in the law firm and later chairman of Securicor Group. Indeed, it was the development of the security company which was soon to fill Peter Smith's time and eventually lure him away from Hextalls to join the Group.

By 1968 Wiggs was following a similar path, working exclusively for Securicor within the confines of Hextalls. His first assignment took him to Ireland to negotiate an agreement on behalf of Securicor with the Irish Transport and General Workers Union. The young man who had never previously been abroad soon found himself living out of a suitcase as he travelled around Africa, providing legal support for local acquisitions.

With the death of Keith Erskine in 1974 and Peter Smith's appointment as group chief executive, Wiggs faced the decision which was to change his career. Asked by Smith to join Securicor, Wiggs weighed up his options and, never one to forego a challenge, agreed to take up the post of overseas director of Securicor Ltd.

His progress was swift, with a move up the ranks to become managing director of Securicor International and a seat on the group board following not long after. The retirement of Peter Smith in 1985, and the appointment of Peter Towle as group chief executive, opened the way for Wiggs' promotion to deputy group chief executive and, in 1988, his final step up the ladder to the group chief executive's office.

and, most recently, has culminated in rigorous management training at the company's dedicated Hartsfield Manor centre, in addition to long-established operational training.

If its people are its most valuable asset, Securicor's name and reputation around the world come a close second, opening doors to new customers and cementing partnerships with organisations across the business spectrum. The Group's lasting commitment to the public good and the unusually large number of relationships it has built with chiefs of government and local authority services, as well as industry leaders, have also proved propitious in securing its reputation as an honourable member of society.

The Group's public image is no less distinguished, with staff expected to look and play the part of professional service providers. While Erskine's demands for a smart appearance and polite manners smacked of paternalism, the result quickly became a part of accepted company culture and, hand-in-hand with careful people management, went far to create the 'one big family' sentiment which draws so many into Securicor's employ and helps them to give of their best.

Such commitment to quality has, in turn, been a huge contributor to Securicor's organic growth — after all, customers choosing a provider of cash services need the assurance of dealing with an operator which will make every endeavour not to lose their money, while those selecting distribution services are looking for a reliable link in the supply chain.

Services initially developed to meet in-house needs, for example vehicle servicing and IT support, are also carefully tuned for internal use before being offered on the external market as known quantities which will supply customers with real, rather than perceived, benefits.

While organic growth is necessary in any field, Securicor has long held the belief that it must be coupled with expansion through acquisition. This, it argues, is the only route to true globalisation and, in modern parlance, the only way to hit the ground running in new markets and geographic sectors.

Much has been bought along the way — most notably in terms of international development, the local cash carrying and guarding operations in the Far East, Africa and the Americas — but the Group has never been slow to admit that an activity has reached its sell-by date. Having condensed the Group's widespread activities into four divisions, Wiggs and his management team continue to look within, weeding out non-core businesses and planting potential profit makers.

Having mastered divisionalisation in 1990, it is now Roger Wiggs' task to take Securicor plc, the result of a 1996 merger of Securicor Group plc and Security Services plc, into the new millennium. Making history from examples of the past, he not only seeks innovation but also expansion into new markets and territories.

His objectives are clear, his mission plan equally erudite: to double margins by turning loss makers into profit providers and investing in already successful operations to increase the percentage of profit on sales. His personal challenge is to see Securicor plc listed on the FT-SE 100.

The company is already well on its way, with a capitalisation of close to £2 billion following the creation of the single plc, a move supporting further forward momentum through a simplified voting structure which is increasing investor interest and, hence, financing options for acquisition and inward investment.

Juxtaposing old with new, the opportunities which Securicor seeks to grasp are prolific. On the basis of the business philosophies and policies which have been tried and tested over the past 60 years, there is no reason to suppose it will not be successful.

■

"Divisionalisation has had the advantages of giving people more responsibility, clarifying reporting lines, driving decisions down through the company and giving individuals ownership of parts of the business"
— Roger Wiggs

■

Advice from the Lawyers

While Roger Wiggs mulled over the business potential of creating a single quoted company and began to consider the internal changes which would be needed to make the most of such a restructure, behind the scenes the group's legal and financial personnel were examining the scheme and finalising every detail.

From a legal and financial standpoint, the greatest concern was to create, within a tax efficient structure, a formula which would

*Nigel Griffiths, Group Legal Director and
Company Secretary*

meet all the aspirations of the different shareholder classes. The task was never going to be simple, but, in conjunction with group legal director and company secretary Nigel Griffiths, teams of lawyers, merchant bankers and stockbrokers were put in place to address the legal and financial implications of the integration.

Cazenove & Co was nominated as overall stockbroker for the transaction, while Lazard Brothers, Securicor Group's merchant bank, and Herbert Smith, a major City law practice familiar with the Group, looked after the interests of Securicor Group and its shareholders. Security Services, as an independent company with its own shareholders, appointed Schroders merchant bank and lawyers Slaughter and May to consider its interests.

After an assessment of the potential benefits of the proposed reorganisation for both companies and after winning board approval for the merger, it was necessary to canvass shareholder opinion. Documentation was prepared, extraordinary general meetings arranged and, after all the hard work, the merger team was rewarded with resounding support from shareholders.

The success of the restructure in business development terms has been reflected in brisk trade in new Securicor shares, but the change has also brought significant benefits to the internal workings of the Group. No longer will there be any likelihood of conflict of interest between different classes of shareholder, nor will there be the need to duplicate effort in producing two annual reports and orchestrating two annual general meetings.

Perhaps the biggest bonuses for those employed within the Group, however, are the employee share schemes which can be offered as a result of the reorganisation. Again, Griffiths' legal department has been instrumental in organising the schemes, which have attracted widespread interest.

Launched at the end of June 1996, the Executive Share Option Scheme offers certain senior staff, both in the UK and overseas, the opportunity to buy shares between 1999 and 2006 at the price quoted on the launch day. A similar scheme had been established in 1983, but was later abandoned due to opposition from certain shareholders who, as the price for their support, insisted that the capital structure should first be sorted out.

The Employee Sharesave Scheme, a first for Securicor, is proving a winner, offering every UK employee with over one year's service an attractive package. Over 5,500 staff have taken up the option to buy shares in three years' time at the market price quoted on 27 June 1996, discounted by 20 per cent.

The scheme, which it is hoped will be repeated on an annual basis, operates in conjunction with Abbey National. Staff who choose to make monthly deposits are assured of a dependable savings environment plus a bonus at the end of the three-year term, which can then be used to buy Securicor shares.

Putting People First

In a labour intensive business, people must always be a top priority, a fact not lost on Securicor despite the scale and scope of its operations. From a standing start in 1935, the Group has grown to employ more than 27,000 staff in the UK and a total of close to 54,000 worldwide.

Caring for the career development and well-being of each individual has, since the early days of Night Guards Limited, been an inherent company value, resulting in a level of staff loyalty and commitment rare in today's big business environment. While there are exceptions to every rule, the majority of Securicor employees spend many years with the Group, stepping on to the corporate ladder the day they arrive and many climbing to great heights before they depart.

Training has consistently been central to personnel policy, opening doors to new opportunities and reinforcing Securicor's professional image. In the late 1940s, a comprehensive programme was set up, covering both induction training and on-the-job supervision for static guards.

Men joined on Mondays, Thursdays and Fridays, spending their first day with the operations manager and the next two being tutored by the duty inspector in the control room. New recruits would be briefed on assignment duties before being despatched in pairs to their first guarding post, accompanied by a sergeant whose role it was to ensure that each guard was competent. The following

■

"Our growth and market position have been achieved as a result of the very strong culture throughout the group"
— Roger Wiggs,
report to employees, 1991

■

■

"We have always been blessed at Securicor with extremely loyal staff who have been the backbone of our progress over the years"

— Roger Wiggs,
report to employees, 1992

■

night involved visits to a number of different assignments with a chief inspector, before a well-earned rest day and an interview with the managing director to assess whether the individual should be offered permanent employment. Once on the payroll, new guards were visited nightly for two weeks by a chief inspector charged with the job of monitoring and reporting their progress.

Such a lengthy and human resource-hungry training scheme could not, however, outlast the surge in business and recruitment of the next decade. Courses were shortened, but augmented by a day visit to experience the work of the Slough branch headed by Robert Peat and later by judo training for those carrying cash.

By the early 1970s, training was once again to the fore, encouraged not only by the internal interest of vice chairman of Securicor Limited, Sir Frederick Delve, former head of the London Fire Brigade, but also the swingeing levy on the company's wage bill imposed by the Road Transport Industry Training Board, a government quango. With a significant amount of money being paid to the board, it was only logical to seek a sizeable training grant through the implementation of thorough courses.

Thus, courses held in London for managers and branch executives were extended from two weeks to four, and later to six weeks, although it should be added that chairman Keith Erskine would only honour the expense on the basis that all trainees and instructors take part in cash-in-transit duties on Thursdays and Fridays, as well as covering a static guarding assignment over the weekends of their stay in London. A policy applauded by local branch managers in need of extra hands, but deplored, if quietly, by many students and instructors.

If Erskine's approach of mixing training with operational duties was somewhat unusual, he did provide excellent aids and facilities including video equipment, a sound-proof recording studio and well-equipped classrooms. Training centres were also established in the provinces to give new recruits both an introduction to the company and specific training in their tasks.

Besides being an advocate of training in general, Sir Frederick also underlined the importance of fire training, pointing out that the company would be scuppered should one of the industrial premises it was hired to protect burn down and the guards be found untrained in fire prevention. During 1971, Sir Frederick proudly announced that 129 staff had attended management seminars and 680 guards had completed basic courses.

His belief in staff development is as widely held within the Group today as it was then: "Training creates a sense of craftsmanship and pride in the job, it builds confidence and defeats boredom. Not only does it result in a satisfied and happy guard but, equally important, in a satisfied customer."

Training took another major step forward following the death of Keith Erskine in 1974. With advice from the Road Transport Industry Training Board, a more formal training scheme, based on the theory of management by objectives, was introduced and endorsed by new chairman and managing director Peter Smith, who made it clear that he wished to offer ambitious staff a management development path and job security, but never promotion to a degree of incompetence.

Operation Hidden Treasure followed, identifying potential managers and ensuring they were given the skills and opportunities to climb the corporate ladder. Building on the company's traditional thesis of promotion from within, in 1975 Smith reported that all branch managers had completed a management course and that places were available for 1,200 supervisory staff to train with a view to further promotion. Job vacancies were posted in every branch and selection boards established to pick the right men and women for the tasks at hand.

By 1977, a staff training centre at The Richmond Hill Hotel was turning out effective branch managers, but the implementation of their management ability was hampered by the rule that all staff undertake cash-in-transit duties at the end of the week. Recognising the problem, Smith changed Keith Erskine's ground rules, releasing branch managers from operational duties.

Further change came with the arrival of a Conservative government in 1979 and the disbanding of the Road Transport Industry Training Board, leaving Securicor in full control of its in-house training need and budget.

■

"Securicor will continue to develop the core attributes of reliability and integrity which we demonstrate throughout our businesses from the most well established to those in the early stages of development"
— Roger Wiggs,
report to employees, 1993

■

■

"I am proud of the quality of management displayed within our operating subsidiaries everywhere and I am constantly impressed by the devotion and enthusiasm of all our staff"

— Roger Wiggs,
report to employees, 1994

■

So developed the firm foundations of Securicor's training activity. No-one is exempt, with new recruits being given extensive induction courses and established staff being offered management or specialist skills development at fully equipped company training centres, as well as ongoing on-the-job training. Employees working in specific businesses such as cash and custodial services also undergo detailed education, both for their own protection and the best service of the customer.

Further up the chain, middle managers are taking part in a programme of Henley Distance Learning at Securicor's Hartsfield Manor executive centre in Surrey, while the Group's directors have all completed the Institute of Directors' Diploma in Company Direction and continue to refine their skills with help from external professionals.

This structured approach, taking into account both generic and divisional requirements, is further augmented by Securicor's membership of the International Management Development Consortium. A group of blue-chip organisations, the consortium's mission is to collectively develop and deliver cost-effective, international and future-focused learning geared to members' requirements. Participation in a similar body dedicated to global issues is also under discussion, while, closer to home, subjects

Management training centre, Hartsfield Manor

such as foreign languages and business cultures are being tackled as a forerunner to improving staff capabilities overseas.

The staff development brief mastered by Peter Williams, head of group training services, is just part of the remit of group personnel director, Peter Humphrey. Based at headquarters in Sutton, he is responsible for personnel policies covering everything from recruitment, payroll and pensions, to training, employment law, health and safety and also in-house communication.

As a lower-quartile payer but with employment costs in excess of £550 million, a major chunk of overall spending, Securicor is keenly aware of the need to maintain tight margins. The security and distribution divisions in particular must motivate their thousands of staff with more than financial remuneration. For many, the freedom of being out on the road and organising one's own working day weighs heavily in the scales against pecuniary gains, while others relish teamwork and the challenge of constantly changing and often demanding situations.

In one aspect, however, all staff are united. Perhaps the most pervasive element across the company, and certainly one which has contributed much to its growth, is the feeling of being part of a large and extended family. Employees describe their work as an integral part of their lives, offering variety, security and companionship. Again, this is a throw-back to the 1940s, when Night Guards and later Securicor hired only ex-servicemen, who brought with them the essence of loyalty, discipline and camaraderie which has since permeated the entire workforce.

With so many long-serving staff as a result, the Group operates an awards scheme for all those with over 15 years' service, presenting them with a company memento, a nominal monetary reward and an invitation to join colleagues, with their partners, for a celebratory dinner. During retirement the bond remains, with the Securicor Old Comrades Association, devised by Peter Smith, organising regional social events and maintaining an interest in the welfare of old friends and their families.

Such interest in staff past and present reflects the altruistic nature of the company's first chairman, Keith Erskine. While

■

"In such a fast-moving environment, I see it as my highest priority to ensure that we have the right management skills to take the business forward and we continue to invest in training at all levels"
— Roger Wiggs, report to employees, 1995

■

■

"If you develop the right people you will win in any business. The hardest task is finding the people in the first place, training them and giving them the right environment and incentives so that they will stay with you"

— Roger Wiggs

■

GUARDIAN
THE SECURICOR MAGAZINE   AUTUMN/WINTER 1993

MAKING THE WORLD A SAFER PLACE
Private prisons ● Tracking car thieves
Pony rides ● Down Whitehall way

some of his schemes were nothing short of bizarre — the Good Reading and Good Music Clubs dreamt up with a view to widening employees' horizons by providing low-cost books and records fell by the wayside — a caring attitude prevailed and is today exemplified by company support for staff involvement in activities such as charitable and community projects. At a more formal level, pension and life insurance schemes are available to all staff, along with professional financial advice from a recommended independent financial advisor.

Benefiting from the concern shown by Night Guards' founders Lord Willingdon and Henry Tiarks, the Schroder Trust today yields a substantial annual sum and is used to help employees and their families in cases of financial hardship, often donating much of its yield to requests from current and ex-employees for help in purchasing medical aids. Initially set up to hold the profits of the founders' shares for the benefit of employees and later buying its own shares, the trust grew from a modest value to a sizeable investment following the sale of Night Guards to Associated Hotels in 1960 and the recognition of Securicor as a solid stock market player in the 1970s and 1980s.

Underpinning the concept of a commercial yet caring community, internal communication has traditionally been an important aspect of company life.

Securicor Guardian, set up in the early 1960s and a communication conduit greatly used by Keith Erskine, ran for many years before being consigned to history after its 100th edition to make way for *Securicor News*, a bi-monthly newspaper distributed throughout the Group. In addition to these company-wide internal publications, each division also has its own communication channels, including magazines, newsletters and information bulletins.

As one old-hand points out, however, there is nothing better for keeping up with the gossip than maintaining contact with long-standing colleagues who once wore a number on the sleeve of their guard's uniforms when they sallied forth from HQ in London and now work in Securicor offices around the world.

Commitment to Charity

Securicor provides a fine example of the concept that charity begins at home. From founder Keith Erskine's commitment to the Multiple Sclerosis Society to today's concerted efforts by staff across the Group to raise funds and contribute to community projects, Securicor has proved its concern for those beyond the boundaries of its business.

The Group operates not only a charitable trust which gives financial support mainly to organisations in the United Kingdom, but also a community action programme designed to lend company experience predominantly to educational institutions, and to business ventures and government sponsored operations.

Set up in 1978, the Securicor Charitable Trust is currently chaired by Anne Munson, Company Secretary – UK Subsidiaries and personal assistant to Securicor group chief executive Roger Wiggs. A trust committee of five executives from across the divisions meets regularly to assess appeals and decide how to disperse funds. From the early days of making just a handful of donations at bi-monthly meetings, the trustees now consider 1,500 requests a year, of which about one in ten is successful. With a total income of about £50,000 a year from covenants made within the Group, the trust normally donates sums of £250 but will occasionally give up to £1,000 to support a particular project.

Charities which consistently find favour include national organisations such as the British Red Cross and a number of cancer concerns including Macmillan Nurses and Marie Curie Cancer Care, as well as hospices, local schools and protected housing schemes for the disabled. While the majority of the trust's work is in the UK, it does make occasional overseas donations, particularly to countries where Securicor's presence is strong.

Besides an ongoing charitable commitment, Securicor has also developed a reputation as a major fund raiser for specific causes. The Multiple Sclerosis Society was always close to the Erskines' hearts after Keith Erskine's wife became involved in a local branch and, more poignantly, following the death of brother Denys from a similar nerve destroying disease.

■

"As a director of a public company I must maximise the value of shares as well as look after our employees and consider the public good."
— Roger Wiggs

■

Keith Erskine chaired the Society's national appeal committee, working with Securicor staff to raise money and provide services such as company transport to give MS sufferers greater mobility. Later support included a company-wide effort in 1981 which raised £33,000 — well over an initial target of £20,000 — to provide a specially equipped ambulance for MS sufferers staying at the Kenninghall holiday home in Worthing.

Securicor's Golden Jubilee in 1985 was marked by a sterling effort for the Save the Children Fund. A target of £100,000 was announced. A lottery with a first prize of a Ford Fiesta car, donated by the Ford Motor Company, went some way towards reaching the goal, assisted by branch activities across the country including everything from a Midsummer Frolic at The Richmond Hill Hotel, to sponsored marathon runs and a cycle ride from John o' Groats to Land's End.

A year of strenuous fund raising was graciously acknowledged in November 1985, when Her Royal Highness the Princess Anne collected cheques worth £125,000 from Securicor chairman Peter Smith at a celebration at The Richmond Hill Hotel.

More recently, a major push for charity in 1993, supported by Roger Wiggs and his management team, benefited the NCH Action For Children charity to the extent of £105,000.

Beyond the bounds of traditional charitable support through financial donations, Securicor maintains its reputation as a good citizen through numerous local and national projects which are co-ordinated and developed within the Securicor Community Action Programme, led by head of group training services Peter Williams.

Senior management enthusiasm, coupled with the Group's strengths in staff numbers and geographical coverage, have proved an ample base on which to build long-term commitment to charitable work.

THE
HISTORY 2

"They wore a smart blue uniform with silver buttons that reminded one of those dashing Hussars in Viennese operettas circa 1913"

– Thus did a client of Night Watch Services describe the first guards to provide property protection against burglars in London's richest residential areas

THE HISTORY

Securicor today has an international reputation not only in the security business, but also in distribution, communications and business services. Back in 1935, however, the story was very different. Registered with a nominal capital of £100, Night Watch Services was formed by the Right Honourable Edward Shortt KC, a barrister and former Liberal cabinet minister. Noting an upsurge of burglaries in the salubrious areas of Mayfair, Hampstead and St John's Wood, Shortt decided the time was ripe to supplement Metropolitan Police services with private security.

The enterprise he formed was modest, limited to external surveillance of private residences and carried out by guards on bicycles. The armed services were the chief source of recruits, a long-lasting policy which assured the company of employees with a strong sense of discipline, loyalty and inherent pride in their appearance.

Indeed, from those early days, image has played a key role in every aspect of the company's business, from individual uniforms to corporate presentation. Shortt sowed the early seeds, embellishing the uniform guard's cap with the cross keys emblem and the motto 'For Thine Especial Safety'.

SECURITY SPECIALISTS
SINCE 1935

While the service was well regarded by its clients, it did not attract enough interest to become a viable commercial concern and Shortt ran out of cash to pay the wages of his one sergeant and three guards. Alarmed at the prospect of losing the protection afforded by Night Watch Services, two of its clients stepped in to fill the breach. Henry Tiarks, a merchant banker and resident of Hampstead, and the Marquis of Willingdon, with a town house in Mayfair, paid £100 for the company. It was more an attempt to keep the service going and the guards in employment than a money-making proposition.

Resistance to paying for services which many felt should be provided by the police limited expansion and, as the outbreak of the Second World War approached and the company changed its name to Night Guards Limited, just 12 patrol guards were employed. Pacifist politician George Lansbury went further, raising the issue of security companies masquerading as private armies – a suggestion which has repeatedly haunted the industry to this day – when he described the guards as representing 'the first faltering steps down a road to fascism'.

The debate was cut short when the country went to war on September 3rd, 1939. Henry Tiarks and Lord Willingdon took up military duties and Night Guards fell into abeyance.

On their return to civilian life in 1945, the partners decided to restart the business. Cultural changes created by the war and an end to the opulence of high society which had marked the 1930s diminished the need for residential guards. Instead, the company moved into industrial security, with a remit to protect factories and commercial buildings. Thus were the foundations laid of the edifice which would become the Securicor Group.

Night Guards' first static guarding contract was won from Vauxhall Motors. The brief was to supply two guards to provide nightly surveillance of the company's spare parts depot in Barnet. With thousands of men being demobilised every week, finding ex-servicemen to take on guarding jobs was not difficult. The emerging commercialism of Night Guards and the need to offer customers honest and able guards gave rise to some of the formal procedures which have lasted the test of time.

Key to the company's reputation for integrity was personnel screening. Applicants had to provide details of 20 years' continuous employment, or an employment history back to their school days, as well as supplying personal references and signing a statement to confirm the information and that they had never been convicted of a criminal offence. Both induction and on-the-job training were also established, again creating a policy which has been continually augmented.

As the business gained pace, further structure was incorporated with the introduction of a firm of auditors to advise on the company's growing financial affairs. A legal suit also alerted the need for a solicitor to be appointed. And so was introduced the man who would have the most significant impact on the development of Securicor, lawyer Keith Erskine.

By 1951, some 170 guards were employed and operations had extended as far as Brentwood, Erith, Welwyn Garden City and Waltham Cross. To meet the rise in running costs, the company increased its capital from £100 to £10,000. On the basis of its activities, Night Guards soon became Security Corps in the public's eye, a name outlawed by the Home Office eager to pacify those who alleged the company was little more than a private army. Following some dextrous thought, the name Securicor was coined and duly registered on January 1st, 1953.

Further growth presaged the appointment of the company's first dedicated salesman, André Verdi, as well as the arrival of Wing Commander Geoffrey Selby-Lowndes as personnel manager and welfare officer. Besides a staff of 360 guards, Securicor could claim 150 guarding contracts covering a total of £350 million worth of property across London.

But, as the company started to make a profit, owners Henry Tiarks and Lord Willingdon found themselves prey to the harsh tax burdens of the day. With the help of Keith Erskine and colleague in the law firm Hextall, Erskine & Company, Peter Smith, an employee trust was set up with the aim of passing ownership from the company's founders to the trust on behalf of Securicor's employees. While its purpose has changed, the trust continues, accruing sums from share dividends which are allocated to staff in need.

Keith Erskine, Securicor's first lawyer

So too did Securicor's employees address their own interests, setting up a Guards' Welfare Committee to administer the collection of 3d a week 'tea money' and later setting up an annual Christmas party for the children of all the staff.

By the close of 1954, Securicor could boast all the facets of a well-organised and healthy company, offering both established services and new additions such as Telecontact, which allowed clients employing their own night watchman to operate a back-up link to Securicor's control room. Further, the company was recognised by industry and commerce as a necessary adjunct to the police force in the prevention of crime, a fact underlined by an invitation to join the Ligue Internationale des Sociétés de Surveillance, a worldwide organisation founded with the objective of exchanging information about industrial security.

The company's prowess was reflected in 1957 with the acceptance by Major Sir Philip Margetson, assistant commissioner of the Metropolitan Police from 1946 to 1957, of a seat on the board and three years later its chairmanship. The appointment did much to boost police confidence in the company as an ally in the fight against crime and was the first of many such relationships, all of which have served Securicor well in providing both expertise and kudos.

The control room at Old Swan House

If Securicor's strength can, in part, be illustrated by the attraction of top government and commercial executives to its upper echelons, its growth over the years must be put down to an ongoing programme of acquisition and diversification which recognises both the emergence and disappearance of potential opportunities.

An agreement with New York-based detective agency Pinkerton's saw the company extend its reach into London's private detective business – a service which was later abandoned – while, in the mainstream, it acquired South Western Security Services in Southampton and Southern Security Services of Reading.

As in any maturing industry, with the concept of acquisition and diversification for growth, comes the corollary of competition. Securicor was not immune. An ex-employee was first into the market with a mobile patrol service registered as the Night Security Company. Able to cover three times as many assignments as Securicor's bicycle patrols, by the late 1950s the company was making a significant indent in Securicor's previously exclusive customer base.

The Armoured Car Company, set up in 1957 along American lines, offered the first cash movements in heavily protected and armoured vans, a service quickly emulated by De La Rue's Security Express subsidiary as wage snatches accelerated through the 1960s. Long-standing market participant Securitas, a Swedish firm operating in England under the Factory Guards name, was also making its mark.

Despite high-profile contracts such as guarding the Ageless Diamond Exhibition at Christies, Securicor had much to do if it was to hold its own in an increasingly active market. By 1959 the number of guards had grown to over 650 but it was proving difficult to recruit further staff of the right calibre. To make matters worse, Securicor made the mistake of raising the wages of the existing guards without increasing charges to customers. An inevitable gloom and despondency descended on the company and, once again, its founders decided it was time to sell.

As the company's legal adviser, Keith Erskine was called in. Always at pains to please his clients he approached his brother, a successful hotelier who had built a London-based hotel company on the legacy left to him in 1944 by the brothers' father, Sir James Erskine. By 1958, Denys Erskine controlled nine hotels in the Associated Hotels group and commanded profits of over £73,000.

The acquisition of Kensington Palace Hotel Limited added to the chain and gave Keith his first chairmanship.

His new position proved propitious as, with funds available for investment, Keith suggested to his brother that Kensington Palace Hotel buy Securicor. It was an audacious proposition but, after much familial disagreement and only the advantage of acquiring Securicor's riverside headquarters, Old Swan House, appealing to Denys, the deal was concluded. In April 1960, Securicor Limited became a wholly owned subsidiary of Kensington Palace Hotel.

Old Swan House, the company's riverside headquarters

On close inspection, however, the company was found to be losing money at a rate of £20,000 a year, a situation which both frustrated and spurred on its new owner. In a familiar burst of energy, Keith swiftly bought out the profitable Night Security business and sheltered the company from negligence claims by arranging an errors and omissions insurance policy covering up to £1 million for a premium of £1,200 a year.

These developments did not, however, solve the company's financial crisis and, as a stock exchange quoted company, it became critical that Kensington Palace Hotel show a better return on its investment, a point not lost on brother Denys. Nor, perhaps, on Keith, who soon left Hextalls for an office in Old Swan House.

Thereafter the building of the Securicor empire gathered speed. Against opposition from both his brother and colleagues, Keith decided to plunge into the cash-in-transit business dominated by the Armoured Car Company. Like so many of his apparently untenable decisions, the purchase of an initial six cash-carrying vehicles was later to prove a sound building block in the construction of the company. In the early 1960s, however, it was a touch-and-go affair as such vehicles had to be licensed to carry cash under the Road Traffic Act. If another carrier already operated in the area covered by a proposed licence, the application had to be heard before a full-scale hearing of the Traffic Commissioners. In characteristic manner, Keith was undaunted, hiring a team of lawyers to chase licence requests through the courts and often appearing in person to argue the case.

Besides giving Securicor access to the cash-in-transit business, the battle for licences also spawned a network of regional offices

– many of them little more than garret rooms – which would later be recognised as another essential element in the foundations of the company.

In the hectic days of 1961, however, the scramble seemed more like a whirlwind tour of the country to Harry Price, the Hextall's lawyer commanded by Keith to open branches anywhere and everywhere.

By the end of the year, 40 offices haphazardly strewn across the country were in operation. The end of National Service conscription provided a pool of potential employees, but for those who succeeded in winning jobs with Securicor their lifestyle was neither settled nor secure. Always eager to keep his finger on the pulse, Keith moved his best staff around the country, often at a day's notice, and was quick to dismiss those who fell short of his expectations, be they professional or personal.

Continuing growth proved extremely costly, however, and, once again, Securicor found itself sailing close to the wind within the Kensington Palace Hotel group. Far in excess of the £25,000 losses predicted by Keith Erskine for 1961, the company in fact lost nearer £200,000, absorbing almost all the hotel group's record profits for the year. Not surprisingly, relations between Keith and brother Denys were strained to the limit. Had they snapped, Securicor would most probably have been up for sale again. Often against his better judgement, however, Denys persevered, providing the solid financial backing of his Associated Hotels group, without which the nascent security firm would have failed.

In his constant struggle to justify the investment in Securicor and his refusal to acknowledge defeat, Keith reported to the directors in March 1962 that, according to his calculations and based on vastly improved performance by the branches, the company would stem its losses by May, adding that the time would then be ripe for a second wave of expansion.

Such forecasts were certainly optimistic and became even more demanding as Securicor fell prey to an increasing number of bandit attacks on its cash-in-transit vehicles. Celebrations for the arrival of the company's 200th armoured vehicle were marred by news of the loss of £10,500 to bandits led by a middle-aged man disguised as a city gent. Erskine moved swiftly to prevent further such attacks and also put up for consideration a number of new ideas including the employment of a third man as cover and an aerosol container in each cash box, which could be activated by a threatened guard to dye notes and render them useless.

The need for all staff to obey strict procedures was also emphasised and forms part of the company's mantra to this day. As the scale and violence of attacks escalated, so too did the company's effort to prevent crime, protecting both its staff and its customers' valuables. Among many of the measures taken in the early 1960s was the installation of a radio communications network. It kept track of cash-in-transit vehicles as well as providing a link to static guards patrolling customer premises. Its success was the catalyst for the development

of Securicor's communications expertise, now reflected in a specialist division and participation in Cellnet, the cellular telephone company.

Among early admirers of the two-way radio network were UK road hauliers, worried by an alarming number of expensive raids. Taking his cue from the Road Hauliers Association, Keith worked with radio equipment supplier Pye Telecommunications to develop the so-called Haulage Emergency Link Protection service, HELP for short. It offered two-way fitted radios connecting drivers to Securicor control rooms for an installation fee of £5 and weekly rental of £2.

Another lasting result of the early bandit attacks was the introduction of bravery awards to staff whose gallantry or meritorious conduct surpassed expected conduct.

So too did the increasing number of attacks spawn new services, in particular the Paypak wage packeting service, which

An early training film pits cash-in-transit guards against the bandits

made customers' wages offices a less attractive proposition than when huge sums of money were delivered for subsequent division. In later years, services such as coin collection and sorting, as well as automatic teller machine replenishment and servicing have also become a mainstay as customers realise the advantages of using a specialist to handle their cash.

Despite increasing volumes of business, however, Keith's 1962 profit forecast proved previous and his triumph did not come until the end of the financial year in September 1963, when he could claim a profit from Securicor of £38,000.

Not content with serving only the UK market and flushed with success, he moved on to phase two of his expansion plans with a vision to create a global concern. A foray into Dublin stalled but, farther afield, a foothold in Malaya opened the way to building a successful business in the Far East, which soon included Hong Kong and Singapore bases and later many smaller operations. Incursions into New Zealand and Australia were less rewarding.

Back at home, activity was equally frenetic, with the acquisition of the Armoured Car Company and the integration of its cash-in-transit services and many of its disciplines and practices – minus the shotguns – with those of Securicor. Among the company's chief attractions was the first purpose-built security centre built in Europe. Located in West Drayton on the outskirts of London, it was put into operation by Securicor in June 1965 and became the model on which a number of other similar centres would be designed. Where original branch locations had been chosen almost randomly, the new security centres were established in large towns with potential for cash-carrying services and formed part of a strategic growth plan.

Prince Charles tours the purpose-built security centre at West Drayton

On the contract front, the

company secured a prestigious arrangement with the Jockey Club to protect racehorses against doping, a contract which gave Securicor a high profile at over 50 racecourse stables and which was only terminated in 1974 when the Jockey Club decided to organise its own security.

Management too welcomed new additions, particularly Sir Frederick Delve, retired chief of the London Fire Brigade, who was persuaded to join the Securicor board to advise on improving the all-round property protection offered by the company, and later Sir Ranulph Bacon, former deputy commissioner of the Metropolitan Police.

Keith Erskine's entrepreneurial spirit was well to the fore as the 1960s unfolded. His next opportunity arose with the spread of computers through the banking, commercial and industrial worlds. Spewing out reams of confidential data such as payroll and banking details, the new technology demanded a secure transport network to move information from central computer locations to regional offices and customers. Erskine was quick to identify the business potential and in mid-1965 launched the Data Transit Service, a fleet of Ford vans driven by young women dressed in air hostess style uniforms. He joked that the venture was a safeguard against the day when all the bandits would be behind bars. Such a day is unlikely to be realised, but not even Erskine could guess at the importance this new service would play in the Group.

Sir Frederick Delve

From this humble beginning grew the UK's leading overnight parcels delivery service, now operated under the Securicor Omega Express banner, as well as international parcel and freight services, a courier service and numerous specialist transport services.

Of equal importance, the 1960s saw Securicor's take-over of the Harmondsworth detention centre near Heathrow Airport, a forerunner to the custodial services it has developed in conjunction with the Home Office, and the launch of its first alarms subsidiary.

On a smaller scale, day-to-day business progressed with the setting up of a guard dog kennels and training centre; establishment of the in-house magazine, *Securicor Guardian*; and a short-lived scheme, doomed not by lack of interest but a shortfall in take up, to operate mobile banking units on Saturdays following the clearing banks' decision to close over the weekend.

The company also played a central role in forming the British Security Industry Association. Its mandate was, and still is, to promote high standards of ethics, service, equipment, screening procedures and training to agreed levels of competence within the industrial security industry. Sir Philip Margetson was unanimously elected as the Association's first chairman, a post which was filled between 1977 and 1981 by former Securicor chairman Peter Smith.

As the business flourished, demand for both internal management and external advisers was unrelenting. Having left Peter Smith in charge of his legal practice when he moved full time to Securicor, Keith decided it was time for Smith to devote all his energies to the interests of the company. Among the young partners who took on a share of Smith's other clients, while he dedicated his career to Securicor, was Roger Wiggs. His days as a lawyer were also numbered, however, and he was quickly whisked away to help Securicor establish an alarms division, before being sent on a lengthy tour which would mark the establishment of independent businesses and partnerships across the African continent.

Also making their way through the company were two young men, Henry McKay and Pat Howes, who are today chief executives of divisions within the Group. Erskine's ability to spot talent as well as the group's consistent policy of promoting from within are recurrent themes throughout this history.

Externally, he augmented the team with the appointment of public relations firm Michael Joyce Consultants, an agency run by Joyce and Nick Hewer which, for some 30 years, successfully counselled the company, managing the image of Securicor and contributing greatly to the strength of the brand name. Indeed, Michael Joyce could probably write a book twice as long as this to record his experiences of the early days of Securicor. The Group is now served by a number of firms which meet the specialised needs of a diversified, international business requiring a wide range of external expertise.

The death of Denys Erskine in 1966 added to the pressures on his brother and underlined the need for exceptionally competent employees at the helm of Securicor. Besides being chairman of Kensington Palace Hotel, Keith also became chairman of Associated Hotels, although its running was left in the experienced hands of Denys's wife and daughter, and his right-hand man, Eric Hollis.

Denys died before Keith could prove the wisdom of his initial investment in Securicor. By 1967, the company was producing 75 per cent of its parent's pre-tax profit and 60 per cent of that of the

Associated Hotels group. In the half year to March, Securicor recorded pre-tax profit of £236,000, against £103,000 at Associated Hotels. Turnover was also growing rapidly, from a base of £500,000 in 1960 to nearly £8 million in 1967.

The picture was not altogether rosy, however, as bandits' methods became ever more ingenious and the company faced its first shotgun attack, followed in March 1968 by the first fatality of a static guard who was battered to death with an iron bar and, in late 1970, the first death of a cash-in-transit guard, coshed as he carried a cash container from his armoured van into a bank on Cornhill.

Potential financial losses also loomed as more contracts were taken on and customers held service suppliers responsible for damage to their premises, a situation defused by lawyer Peter Smith when a Securicor patrolman, upset following a row with his girlfriend, deliberately started a fire and faced a charge of causing £615,000 worth of damage.

Contrary to legal precedent and after a protracted court battle, the House of Lords finally accepted a contract clause which excluded the company from responsibility for acts of its employees which could not have been foreseen and avoided with all due diligence of the company. Called the 'Mad Clause' by

Hextall's lawyers, Smith's contract limitation made legal history and allowed the entire industry to breathe a sigh of relief.

Such problems did not deter Erskine from the pursuit of his ambition to create a £100 million turnover company by 1976 – unfortunately he did not live to see the target achieved just a year later. At the end of the 1968 financial year, however, Securicor was out-classing the hotel companies.

By all accounts, the 1960s were memorable years in the building of Securicor. In 10 years under the stewardship of Keith Erskine and by dint of his drive, imagination and ability to inspire loyalty in his staff, the company had grown from obscurity to lead the industrial security field.

UK business was booming, with additional high-profile, albeit non-profitable, work pouring in from airlines threatened by terrorist attack. A strike by postal workers in January 1971 gave an immediate fillip to Securicor's delivery service, while decimalisation in February of the same year filled the company's security centres with cash waiting to be deposited after the necessary closure of retail banks for four days. The detective division formally recognised the small army of women which it hired as store detectives and the company renewed its efforts in the security consultancy arena with the launch in 1971 of a dedicated consultancy division.

Overseas, security services in the Far East were well-established and the company's African adventure, in the capable hands of Roger Wiggs, prompted the formation of a new subsidiary called Securicor Global. Entrées into various island countries, a temporary obsession of the chairman, came to nothing but did add to the company's international business acumen.

Europe proved a hard nut to crack but, in his inimitable style, Erskine was reluctant to let an opportunity pass without first testing all the possibilities. False starts in countries as far flung as Malta, Cyprus and Norway did not put him off, but it was not until after his death that Securicor could claim victory in Europe.

Despite these heroic failures, overseas business contributed £3 million to a total 1971 turnover of £27 million. Group profits for the year climbed from £913,000 to break the £1 million barrier at

£1.1 million, 80 per cent of which was generated by Securicor and just 20 per cent by interests in the hotel industry. As in earlier years, the company's minimal losses on cash-carrying contracts kept insurance premiums to a minimum.

While money was coming into the company, however, it was poorly managed, owing, in great part, to Erskine's dislike of accountants. His declaration that he had disposed of the last of the company's money men sounded warning bells to many of his colleagues and those who would follow in his footsteps but, as usual, he was not to be contradicted and, with the promise of a computer to smooth the way, the financial department was thrown into chaos from which it would not be relieved until the arrival of Peter Smith as chief executive and Eric Hollis as financial director. Hollis quickly recognised the size of his task and set about the complete restructuring of the company's financial operations. Essential and wide-ranging controls were installed and in a short space of time a much stronger foundation was put in place, one that would support Securicor's growth in the years ahead. For this, the company remains indebted.

Of more immediate importance, however, was the need to rethink the odd juxtaposition of Securicor's business with that of the hotel group. After much board-level debate, it was decided that the hotel group should be sold as a going concern. A buyer was found and the capital which accrued to Securicor did much to help it reap the rewards of a growing security market and to fund diversification into Europe. Still better, as Keith liked to point out, no sooner had the money been deposited than it earned 14.5 per cent interest, more than the profits of the hotels with none of the problems.

The sale allowed Securicor to rise like a phoenix from the ashes, gaining not one but two listings on the London Stock Exchange as the publicly-quoted Associated Hotels Limited became Securicor Group Limited and Kensington Palace Hotel Limited took on the mantle of Security Services Limited. Free of non-core businesses, Erskine set to work again, realigning his management structure to reflect the decentralisation policy he had adopted in 1970 and which divided the country into zones, areas, sub-areas and branches. At the top of the company, Sir Philip Margetson was marginalised with the title Honorary President, allowing Erskine to step into his post as both chairman and managing director.

The years which followed were challenging as industry battled with ever-changing government pay policies and staff shortages hit an all-time high. With judicious pay planning, Securicor held its own, even picking up extra guarding work as power workers and coal miners left their premises to join national strikes. There was no despondency in the City when Securicor announced a 24 per cent rise in profit to £1.7 million, on turnover of £38 million for the year to September 1973.

It was not long after this success against all odds that Keith Erskine met sudden death on April 23rd, 1974, the result of a car accident during a holiday in Scotland. While family, friends and staff mourned the loss of such a vivacious soul, Securicor stood proudly in memory of his name, enthusiasm, determination and entrepreneurial spirit.

That year marked the end of an exciting era, but only the beginning for Peter Smith who, recommended by Erskine before his death, was elected to the role of chairman and managing director of Securicor at an extraordinary board meeting held on May 3rd, 1974.

His inheritance held much potential but also posed some perilous business problems. A review of service divisions highlighted a lack of consistent profitability in the alarms and cleaning businesses. Under new management, the former continued to founder but retained a position in the company's portfolio which would act as a base for growth in later years under the able guidance of security expert Peter Towle. The latter was eventually disbanded. Despite holding a royal warrant as cleaning contractor to Buckingham Palace, the service found it difficult to recruit and screen staff to the security levels demanded by Securicor.

Elsewhere, the parcels division was in danger of becoming a victim of its own success. Industrial unrest in the public sector led many companies to turn to private firms to distribute goods and

Peter Smith became Chairman and Managing Director in 1974 following Erskine's death

Securicor was all but overwhelmed with parcels. Again, it was new management recruit Towle who was given responsibility for rationalising and developing the division.

On a more personal note, and in the same vein as Peter Smith had been Keith Erskine's right-hand man, Roger Wiggs was singled out by Smith to join him from Hextall's and take on the challenges and mixed fortunes of Securicor's overseas division, while retaining responsibility for the Group's legal, contractual and insurance issues. After his first full year as chairman and managing director, and despite rampant inflation, Smith could report an increase in pre-tax profit from £2.63 million to £2.76 million on turnover growing 32 per cent to £61 million for the 12 months ended in September 1975.

His efforts to develop an effective reporting and communication structure and Operation Survival, which sought savings across the company – not least tightening security procedures to avoid losing money to the bandits – had paid off. With existing business and internal staffing matters under control, Smith laid out the acquisition and diversification policy which has turned Securicor into an international service provider, more than justifying his decision to invest only in ventures complementary to the core industrial security business.

From the initial acquisition of Ford dealership Chiswick Garage, the company's strength in vehicle supply, servicing and bodywork building grew unremittingly. Business-to-business services were augmented with the addition of The Richmond Hill Hotel, The Hylands Hotel and later The Richmond Gate Hotel, while the parcels delivery service grew quickly under Towle's leadership to represent one quarter of UK turnover by 1977. The late 1970s and 1980s were also formative years for the Group's communications business as advances in technology created a global market for cellular telephony. With its long experience in radio networks, Securicor was well placed to take advantage of emerging demand for mobile telecommunications and, in Peter Towle, had a man of vision who foresaw the potential of joining forces with British Telecommunications to form the highly successful Cellnet cellular network. The company's traditional industrial security business was further expanded through the acquisition of competitors such as Birmingham-based Mint Security and alarms specialists Ashley Associates and RCA Alarms Systems, with its established Granley product range.

Geographical diversification was equally vibrant and, having vacated his desk at Hextall's in 1975, Roger Wiggs was soon in charge of an overseas empire employing 8,000 staff in 16 countries. Europe remained a difficult market to penetrate, but was more clearly understood following the appointment of Chris Shirtcliffe, now group finance director, as European finance manager.

By mid-1979, Smith had completed five years as chairman of Securicor Group, Security Services and Securicor Limited, of which he was also managing director. Trading results for 1978 showed record profits of £5.4 million on turnover of £121 million and, mindful of the vacuum which followed the death of his predecessor, Smith decided to spread the management burden among his colleagues.

Eric Hollis was nominated to take on the managing directorship of Securicor Limited and Peter Towle became director of UK operations, furthering a career which was ultimately to lead to his appointment as group chief executive.

With confidence in his management team, Smith decided to reorganise along both regional and operational lines. The security services, freight and parcels, transport, communications and alarms, and overseas divisions which emerged were to be the forerunners of today's operating units within the Group.

The 1980 financial year ended with Group profits up 15 per cent at £7.9 million and the New Year was marked by a tribute to Smith with the award of an OBE for his services to the security industry. Indeed, despite the set-backs of slow economic recovery across the UK and increasingly vicious and costly bandit attacks on Securicor's cash-in-transit vans, the Group's finances continued to prosper. By 1985, the commercial strategy generated a 13 per cent profit rise to £10.1 million, on turnover rising 7 per cent to £247 million at Security Services. Securicor Group

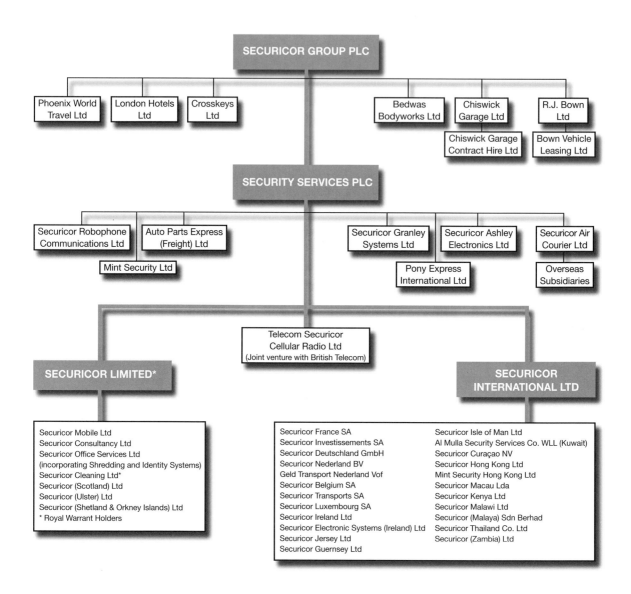

SECURICOR GROUP PLC

Phoenix World Travel Ltd

London Hotels Ltd

Crosskeys Ltd

Bedwas Bodyworks Ltd

Chiswick Garage Ltd

R.J. Bown Ltd

Chiswick Garage Contract Hire Ltd

Bown Vehicle Leasing Ltd

SECURITY SERVICES PLC

Securicor Robophone Communications Ltd

Auto Parts Express (Freight) Ltd

Mint Security Ltd

Securicor Granley Systems Ltd

Securicor Ashley Electronics Ltd

Securicor Air Courier Ltd

Pony Express International Ltd

Overseas Subsidiaries

Telecom Securicor Cellular Radio Ltd
(Joint venture with British Telecom)

SECURICOR LIMITED*

Securicor Mobile Ltd
Securicor Consultancy Ltd
Securicor Office Services Ltd
(incorporating Shredding and Identity Systems)
Securicor Cleaning Ltd*
Securicor (Scotland) Ltd
Securicor (Ulster) Ltd
Securicor (Shetland & Orkney Islands) Ltd
* Royal Warrant Holders

SECURICOR INTERNATIONAL LTD

Securicor France SA
Securicor Investissements SA
Securicor Deutschland GmbH
Securicor Nederland BV
Geld Transport Nederland Vof
Securicor Belgium SA
Securicor Transports SA
Securicor Luxembourg SA
Securicor Ireland Ltd
Securicor Electronic Systems (Ireland) Ltd
Securicor Jersey Ltd
Securicor Guernsey Ltd

Securicor Isle of Man Ltd
Al Mulla Security Services Co. WLL (Kuwait)
Securicor Curaçao NV
Securicor Hong Kong Ltd
Mint Security Hong Kong Ltd
Securicor Macau Lda
Securicor Kenya Ltd
Securicor Malawi Ltd
Securicor (Malaya) Sdn Berhad
Securicor Thailand Co. Ltd
Securicor (Zambia) Ltd

Securicor Group's operational family tree, as revised September 1985

showed a profit gain of 11 per cent to £12.8 million, on turnover advancing 6 per cent to £284 million.

On reaching another personal milestone, however, Smith announced on his 65th birthday that he would relinquish his executive responsibilities for the Group and Security Services, continuing as non-executive chairman of both companies. The appointments of Peter Towle as group chief executive and Roger Wiggs as his deputy ended Peter Smith's successful leadership of the Group, opening new doors for his colleagues and the businesses which he passed on to them.

Towle added a further dimension to the management brief during his three years as group chief executive. Besides overseeing growth across the Group, he took a close look at its finances, introducing regular budget reviews as fierce competition required a careful eye to be kept on the bottom line and ensuring that his successor, Roger Wiggs, took responsibility for a company not only brimming with ideas, but also one with a healthy balance sheet.

Keith Erskine looks on as a control room sergeant explains operations to Prince Philip

But there was much to be done if the company was to continue its strong performance through the new decade and into the twenty-first century. Instead of adding to the lumbering giant's load, however, Wiggs took an early decision to break-up the company and restructure its key lines of business into independent divisions able to respond more nimbly to market demands.

Five clearly defined divisions were crafted from the less formal business lines of the limited company. Obvious candidates were the security and parcels distribution operations. To these were added the burgeoning communications division, initially a supplier of services designed to meet internal needs, but soon to become a market force in its own right; the transport division, bringing together the Group's expertise in fleet management, bodywork manufacture and vehicle dealerships; and, finally, the special services division, an amalgamation of the hotel, recruitment and travel agency interests which had developed in a somewhat *ad hoc* fashion to support the core businesses of security and parcels.

The stories of these divisions, which in 1991 were reduced to four with the joining of transport and special services in a business services division, are told elsewhere in this book. Their growth, however, owes as much to Roger Wiggs' foresight and later his guiding hand as to the success of their products and services. In financial terms, his tenure has seen Group profits rise from £27.3 million in 1988 to £107.4 million in 1996, on turnover rising from £446 million to £1.26 billion – a far cry from Keith Erskine's 1962 promise of a small profit on a turnover target of £2 million.

THE
BUSINESS
MAKERS

3

Keith Erskine: from autocrat to altruist

Genius, visionary, eccentric, autocrat and family-man, Keith Erskine was all of these and more. Without his extraordinary talents and mercurial ways, Securicor would not have become the household name it is today.

But behind the often brusque and commanding facade, lurked a sense of personal insecurity which drove Erskine to strive for success, and a compassion for his fellow men which generated lasting loyalty and comradeship throughout the company.

Born in 1907, Keith Erskine was one of twins, the last children in a family of one daughter and four sons. Neither of the so-called 'twinnies' showed much enthusiasm for sport, but both were academically bright and often whiled away spare time reading the *Financial Times* and preparing a portfolio of shares which they would follow day by day. By the age of 13, Keith was advising his father on investments and so successful was he that his father handed over his portfolio to his son.

School years started badly when Erskine ran away from Westminster School, unable to cope with being bullied by other boarders. But he returned as a day-boy and proved himself a scholar of some merit, progressing to university to study law. An early brush with politics when his father James Erskine was elected an independent Conservative MP came to nought when Keith sought, but failed to win, his candidature in 1929.

His father had resigned his parliamentary seat with the intention of devoting his working life to a small hotel business he was building on the back of the acquisition of The Eccleston Hotel. It was this almost hobbyist endeavour which was to lead to merger with the Associated Hotels group, inherited by the eldest Erskine brother, Denys, on Sir James's death. By then it was not only successful in its own right, but also provided Keith with a constant flow of legal work.

After qualifying as a solicitor in 1933, Erskine set up a one-man law practice, which he was to operate for a year before joining a partnership. By 1935 he was again setting up his own firm, in which he practised until the outbreak of war.

At 32, Erskine joined the Army, serving in both Europe and the Middle East. These were formative years in all respects. Not only did Keith become engaged to his future wife Audrey, a WRNS officer, but also, and equally important, he discovered much about the motivation and leadership of men which was to stand him in good stead in his business career.

Remembering his divisional commander during the Italian campaign, Keith noted his practice of setting out every morning on a mission to visit hundreds of his troops. 'He would come back with some good ideas to pass on to his staff. I suggest that that typified the best kind of leadership when it gave scope to others to state their views,' Erskine recalled.

Later, he wrote: 'What struck me was how few orders were given, yet there was 100 per cent communication. From long sharing of stress and danger, everyone knew what had to be done. If a man was killed, there was always someone to take his place. This teamwork was made much easier by the almost total absence of snobbery. No-one gave a damn what school one came from – it was how one stood up to it that mattered. Ever since, I have dreamed of recapturing this attitude in civilian life.'

Returning from the war, Erskine again took up his legal business, amalgamating with the firm which was to become Hextall Erskine & Company in 1954. Soon joined by Peter Smith, he worked diligently to win potential clients and it was in this constant quest to please clients that he acquired Securicor, with backing from his brother's hotel business.

Making himself managing director, Keith started his career as a business magnate. Variously called The Governor, Father and Mastermind, the nickname which stuck was KE.

His philosophies were many and varied, often leaving colleagues startled by the turns he would take. With a telephone close at hand by day and night, KE would command his empire while, at the start of every day, he would hold post conferences, during which he would gather his staff around his desk and quiz them on every aspect of their work, as well as using the time to project his own ideas – the last thing ever to be mentioned was the daily post bag.

Indeed, he is remembered as much for his mercurial character as the business success he generated on the strength of

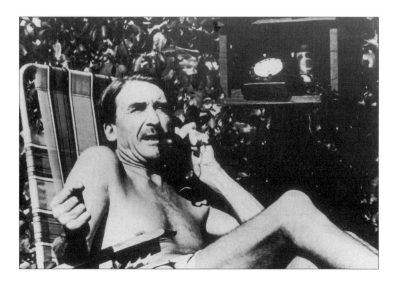

often erratic, but always entrepreneurial, ideas. While KE in fact eschewed letters and memoranda, the telephone was his lifeline and no-one's privacy was guaranteed once their talent had been spotted. Not a man to tolerate incompetence, KE was, by turn, a caring employer and an autocrat, commanding his troops, chivvying them along and, ultimately, handing out dire penalties to those who did not conform. To disagree with him meant instant demerit, but to change his mind through the subtle art of letting him believe the change to be his own idea was a useful ploy.

Early on he preached belief in Henry Ford's philosophy of seeking a small profit on a large and increasing turnover. This concept was central to his plans when KE announced that Securicor would operate as a mutual company, the first of his many departures from normal commercial practice. Without consulting shareholders, he announced his intention to limit Securicor's UK pre-tax profits to five per cent of turnover in any five-year period, declaring Securicor Limited a self-styled mutual company dedicated to the well-being of its customers, shareholders, staff and the common good. With promises of lower prices, improved return on investment, higher pay and adherence to government guidelines on prices and incomes, KE drew up the virtuous circle from which all would benefit – not least Securicor through the amount of media interest the announcement generated. So taken was he by his own idea that the company name emblazoned on all its vehicles was soon annotated to declare 'Securicor Cares'. While the mutual company status has since been dropped, many of its principles remain in force today.

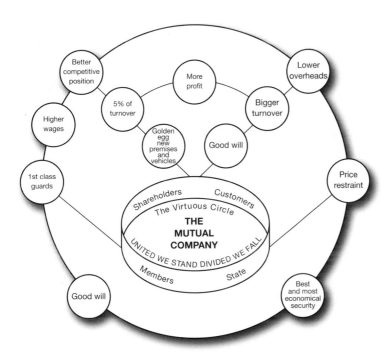

Many of KE's philosophies were dreamt up on holiday, sometimes being communicated by cryptic telexes before his return. One such announced:

In future we shall call ourselves an Ipcamocracy. The suffix -cracy is derived from the Greek word kratia, meaning power or rule. Hence we have well-known uses of the suffix as follows:

Democracy – rule by the people

Autocracy – rule by one man

Aristocracy – rule by privileged order, originally the best people

Bureaucracy – rule by departments of state in the Civil Service.

In Securicor's Ipcamocracy, Ipca stands for:

I – involvement by all

P – participation by all

C – contribution by all

A – achievement by all.

So absorbed was he with this new way of thinking that he eulogised in a letter to the directors about involvement being fostered by good leadership, bringing men into the confidence of management so that the company's objectives could be clearly explained. So the mnemonics multiplied and led to the setting up of Pipdics – Policy, Priorities, Drive and Impetus Committees.

In 1969 followed so-called football teams, which divided operational branch staff into teams and gave each member managerial duties in addition to their everyday work. KE listed five aims he expected the teams to achieve: development of management potential in every member; increased efficiency; improved security; closer customer relations; and enlarged sales. Some 19 teams were initially fielded and an elaborate system of awarding merits was devised, depending on everything from punctuality to mileage saved on cash-in-transit trips. The winners' bonuses, paid weekly over four weeks, amounted to £6 for the captain, £4 for the vice captain and 50 shillings for other members. Despite the quantity of paperwork and analysis involved, the scheme was extended to cover the whole country, with the responsibilities of each team member laid down by KE's Spom – Security, Planning, Organisation and Method – department and it was only withdrawn when decentralisation made its management impractical.

Job titles were considered all important, with supervisors being termed trainers, on the grounds that guards would welcome training to the same degree that they disliked supervision. At an extreme, KE adopted the management philosophy of New York University Professor of Management, Peter Drucker, giving himself the title of chief helper, while branch managers became branch helpers and the job of carer was introduced for those who handled customer complaints.

Influences came from both KE's literary background and contemporary business. He was apt to quote the likes of Tolstoy and Shakespeare, the latter lending him from *Henry V* a description of how men should work within Securicor:

"... there must be no pride of place, no haughtiness of rank, no intoxication of success, no impatience of intellect, no satisfaction of self, no coldness of feeling and no withholding of love."

He endorsed the words of Yehudi Menuhin when he said:

"Discipline is summoned from inside, never from outside and love means service of the highest kind."

After reading *Up the Organisation* by the head of Avis Car Hire, KE often quoted the book as a reminder to management staff not to succumb to the life of plenty:

"Executive offices should be like Trappist cubicles, but the typists pool should look like a Turkish harem."

Coupled with the constant outpouring of new ideas was an urgent need to communicate them to all Securicor staff. Hence KE's preoccupation with the company newsletter launched in December 1960 and later the issue of posters bearing his messages which would be put up in every branch. *The Guardian* in-house magazine provided a further channel, but by far the most ambitious scheme was the recording of video films which were distributed to all the branches for viewing at so-called Beer and Communications get-togethers.

In the first of many monthly issues of the magazine, KE outlined his targets for the company reorganisation programme, both praising existing efforts and demanding more. The publication's purpose of boosting morale was met, but how much of the classical-style prose which KE liked to inject was understood by the rank and file is another matter.

Articles were often instructive in tone, but KE also used *The Guardian* and subsequent in-house publications to open his heart and ask forgiveness for his shortcomings.

At the end of 1962 he wrote of the old guard of staff who had been with him since the start: 'I have driven you, urged you and doubtless there were moments when you wished I had never been born – but you never failed me. If I asked you for turnover, you went out and got it. If I asked you for profitability, you managed your own typing and all did night guard duty – but you got it.'

And to staff old and new he wrote: 'Old guard, young guard, I raise my glass to you. I take back any harsh things I might have said about you. One of my many failings is that I am just not good at praising people – but reluctantly I have to admit that no skipper had a finer team.'

Among his less endearing features was the inability to accept criticism, which usually led to the early departure of the critic, a dismissive approach to ideas not of his own making, or defensive and often aggressive answers to comments which he perceived as slighting his judgement. Thus did many staff find themselves out of a job, as did the company sometimes lose out when KE took umbrage at competitors' activities, immediately setting out to trounce them almost regardless of business sense.

It was in this spirit that he fought to prove wrong his brother's early assertion that Securicor was unsuccessful and showed little promise. His desire for total control of all around him was also at the heart of his violent dislike of union membership to which he had, ultimately, to concede, although he never took the part of company negotiator, preferring to allot the task to Peter Smith.

Where Securicor was concerned, it was evident that KE would stop at nothing in pursuit of success. Tackling both little and large conundrums, in 1961 he changed the company motto to 'Vigilant and Valiant' before addressing the accusation of running a private army by abandoning police-style job titles, altering uniforms to distinguish them more clearly from the Metropolitan Police and setting up regional boards to foster good relations with both local commerce and police forces.

Such sweeping gestures, made overnight and with little concern for the immediate bedlam they would cause, were an Erskine trademark and an indication of his business thinking. While a quick revision of the early years of Securicor suggests a leader with little business policy and even less ability to plan, beneath the apparent carelessness was a mind focused on every aspect of the business and a courage and conviction to make instant change if something or someone was perceived not to be working to best effect.

The Erskine home, Beech Hurst in Kingswood, Surrey, was both a family retreat for KE's children and a business parlour in which he hosted frequent staff and client parties. Known as a generous and congenial host, KE would regale his guests with anecdotes and humorous stories, demonstrating a side of his character unknown to those who met him only in the office. This interest in others also helped him to persuade many top-ranking services staff to join the company board, adding to the company's prestige and its reputation in the City. Likewise, KE's care and concern involved the company in a number of charitable works, such as its long-term involvement with the Multiple Sclerosis Society.

Keith Erskine's home was the venue for frequent staff and customer parties

Conversely, however, he had no tolerance for activities or character facets which he disliked. A non-drinker himself, he abhorred those who drank too much, was always willing to fire those who smoked and despised anyone in his employ who he considered overweight. A keen swimmer and walker, KE would often test his colleagues' physical prowess.

Robert Peat, a member of personnel staff at head office, recalled: "An invitation to join KE in a walk, especially if he put his hand on your shoulder, caused a certain involuntary tensing of the stomach muscles and a lightning review of recent events and one's implication in them. Cynics declared their ability to forecast the outcome from the outset. If KE turned left, the walk would continue along the Embankment, over Chelsea Bridge, through Battersea Park and back over Albert Bridge. Such a walk ended by an offer of a transfer to sales or a suggestion that greater opportunities were to be found elsewhere.

"A walk in an anti-clockwise direction might be a short one through Embankment Gardens and back. This would be one chosen for floating a new idea for your comment or an attempt to draw out an opinion about a colleague. If the walk extended over

Albert Bridge, through Battersea Park and back via Chelsea Bridge it might be to test your fitness, for KE walked at a brisk pace and would terminate with a warning that being overweight or lacking in exercise could end in disaster for both your health and future employment."

As the company expanded through the early 1970s, however, KE continued in his unique management style and it was not until after his death that the problems of such a single-minded, hands-on approach in a large company really emerged.

That said, his flair and entrepreneurial enthusiasm were pivotal in keeping Securicor alive and growing in its early years. Concluding his address to 2,000 staff and friends gathered in St Paul's Cathedral for a memorial service in Keith Erskine's honour, prebendary of the cathedral and chaplain to Securicor, Francois Piachaud, spoke of the lasting memories which would endure for all who had known or worked with this remarkable character: "To the mercy and love of the eternal God in Christ and the Spirit we commit him. Let us commit ourselves likewise and let us pray that in days to come men may say with gladness, as they said about Christopher Wren, *'Lector, si monumentum requiris, circumspice'* – if you seek his monument, look about you."

The Inheritance

The unexpected death of Keith Erskine in April 1974 proved a pivotal point in the development of Securicor. Erskine's belief in his own ideas, while often tending to arrogance, coupled with an expansive vision, had certainly done much to build the original security business and acted as a catalyst for diversification into new areas.

Securicor would not be the group it is today without the imagination and energy instilled by Erskine, but there is little doubt that had he continued to reign in the supreme manner he favoured, the business would have spiralled out of control and, ultimately, out of existence. The company structure and internal functions which he left behind were by no means in line with what was considered best business practice.

Peter Smith: a stabilising influence

"We were all stunned by the news of Keith's death: one minute he was there and the next minute he wasn't. All the phones stopped ringing and people felt lost and fragmented. My appointment as chairman was a daunting prospect. I thought of all the great men on our board, recruited from a wide spectrum of achievement, most of whom didn't know me from Adam.

"There was no time to plan anything. There was my law practice, there was Securicor, there were a lot of people who had given a large part of their lives to building up the company. So when people came up to me and said, look, KE was a great eccentric but the one thing he didn't leave behind was a management team to replace him, I had two reactions. First, I was terribly flattered to be asked to take on the job and, second, regardless of personal inclination, if people want you to do something and they are all worried stiff as to what's going to happen because the captain has suddenly fallen off the bridge, if you've got any sense of duty at all, you do it."

Where Keith Erskine had moved on from Hextall, Erskine & Company to run Securicor, Peter Smith followed, but with no intention of trying to imitate his predecessor and every intention of solidifying the company's achievements to date and creating a firm foundation for future growth.

With the help of vice chairmen Sir Frederick Delve and Sir Richard Jackson, he brought all his experience of working behind the scenes at Securicor to bear, realising immediately the need to develop a strong management team and get a grip on the company's chaotic accounting department. The latter was tackled by Eric Hollis, who joined Securicor as financial director with long experience working within the hotel group. The creation of a management structure was handled through the appointment of regional managers and a renewed commitment to training, which would give staff the ability and motivation to pursue a clear career path towards senior management.

Monthly meetings of the nine regional managers gave the board a good indication of profit and loss activities and proved an instant success. Managers could discuss problems with their peers and head office directors, while Smith could communicate effectively to the entire workforce, building up the trust and loyalty which would be needed to carry the company through worsening depression in world economies. In the quest for competent management, Smith was persistent, launching operation Hidden Treasure which, for many years, would help to identify staff with ambition and ability who could be trained for senior positions.

Such examples of Smith's work paint a very different profile to that of his predecessor and indeed their lives were poles apart. Born in 1920, Smith lived above the surgery of his father's dental practice in South London. He attended St Paul's School, but left at 16 on discovering that colour blindness limited his prospects of following in his father's footsteps. Instead he turned to the law, securing articles with a lawyer who was a patient in his father's practice. By the age of 17 he was running Bullcraig and Davis's Poor Person's legal aid scheme, handling numerous divorce cases. Before he could complete the necessary five-year qualifying period, however, war broke out and Smith joined the Army, spending the next seven years with the artillery and taking part in the 1943 thrust up from Sicily through Europe.

Looking back on his experience in the Army, Smith ranks it as one of the most valuable factors influencing his life. His service alongside regular officers taught him the merit of calmness and the ability to generate confidence in times of stress. On the battlefield, good leadership stood out in bold relief and imprinted a lasting impression on the mind of the young officer.

Returning in 1946 to civilian life and the law firm he had left, Smith resumed his training, winning admission to the legal profession as a solicitor in February 1948 and a salary of £400 a year. Seeing no prospect of being offered a partnership in the firm, however, he sought new pastures and put his name on the Law Society's employment register.

Three days later, Smith had his first encounter with Keith Erskine, who offered him the opportunity to run the conveyancing department of his London law firm for the princely sum of £600 a year. Within weeks of joining Hextall, Erskine & Company in July 1951, Smith was to realise the genius, energy and commitment of his new employer when he was sent to help evict squatters from a property belonging to Denys Erskine. Not content with the usual battery of bailiffs, Erskine insisted Smith climb over neighbouring rooftops and drop through a skylight to escort the unwanted tenants off the premises.

This was just the first of many unusual incidents which Smith experienced while working with the Erskine family. Hours were often long and the work demanding, but there was never an uneventful day. As he recalls: 'I knew I had met an extraordinary man. He had a great capacity for cutting through problems in an eccentric way.'

Unlike many, Smith stayed the course until Erskine's death, when he took up the reins and developed the Group to new proportions. In contrast to his predecessor, the in-coming chief executive adopted a policy of using the talents of those around him and persuading external experts to join the fold, rewarding loyalty with caring management and career opportunities. Far from the interventionist approach of Erskine, Smith modestly describes his role as chairman as 'the man with the oil can'.

He retired as chairman in March 1995, but retained many links with the company, not least the presidency of the Securicor Old Comrades Association.

In a final message to staff, Peter Smith looked back at his 12 years as group chairman, saying: "In recalling the enormous strides which the group has taken, with turnover now measured in hundreds of millions of pounds instead of tens of thousands, our workforce numbered in tens of thousands instead of one or two hundred, and with all the immensely varied operations established across the world, I am amazed that all this has grown from just a few static guards operating in London. Perhaps the explanation lies in a single common thread which, I like to think, links together all the intervening years. Its embodiment is the family spirit embracing dedication, devotion to duty, friendship and compassion, which has always seemed to me to characterise those who work in Securicor, no matter at what level, and whose untiring efforts have earned our success and justified our boast that Securicor cares."

Peter Towle: building for the future

While his tenure as group chief executive was shorter than that of either of his forerunners, Peter Towle contributed to the development of Securicor in no less significant part than Peter Smith or Keith Erskine.

With long experience in the security business, a singular ability to focus on the task in hand and a fascination for technological development, Towle proved to be the right man, in the right place at the right time when he joined the board of Securicor Limited in the new role of special services director in April 1976. Not one to waste a moment, he tackled problems head-on, looking first at their roots in management, financial or market weakness and then creating divisional reorganisation plans which would weed out trouble-spots and prepare the ground for growth.

Indeed, by early 1977, Towle was able to announce to the press a restructure of the parcels service and delineate a clearly defined range of services covering both the UK and continental Europe. By then carrying 1,000 tons of parcels every 24 hours, the need for careful organisation and management of the parcels division had become paramount. But supporting the growing business was no mean feat.

As Towle explained to the assembled journalists: "Our parcels and data handling services have grown by over 30 per cent each year and now represent a quarter of UK turnover. There is a real problem in keeping up with the expansion rate of this very special service. Larger terminals and branches are always being required, the number and size of vehicles grows steadily and, even in these difficult times, there are about a thousand new jobs created in Securicor every year for men and women with the right background and attitude."

A year later, it was not only staff and premises which were at a premium, but also articulated freight vehicles. These were brought in to underpin the new Securicor freight service, called 2/50, which was designed by Towle and his team to cater for the growing bulk parcels market. The step was bold, using most of the proceeds of a rights issue.

Up and running by 1979, the 2/50 service was built on a dedicated branch network and management structure and offered two-day delivery of individual packages weighing up to 50 kg. However, while extremely successful in attracting customers wanting to distribute heavier goods, the service duplicated much of the effort already expended in the parcels distribution business. When the differentiator of parcel weight also proved minimal, the separate services were once again reunited to form a single, robust distribution enterprise.

At the other end of the spectrum, Towle added the Pony Express same-day, door-to-door motorcycle courier business to the Group when it was offered for sale by Air Call. A loss-maker for its previous parent, Securicor Pony Express was quickly turned around by then managing director Richard Benson.

The communications business received no less attention from its new mentor. Towle's firm and, at the time, relatively unusual belief that technological developments would open massive new markets for radio and later cellular communications, called for a reorganisation which would leave this sector able to take advantage of all that lay ahead.

While so many subscribed to the theory that the car phone was only an executive gimmick, Towle's vision was rewarded when the Post Office implemented and upgraded its radio phone service with automatic dialling in 1980, making the sale of car phones to a much wider audience a reality. Towle upped the stakes, building a specialist sales force and pressing on with the installation of radio telephones in Securicor's own fleet of vehicles as well as those of subscribers to its Relayfone service. It was this experience and market presence which would speed the Group's move into cellular communications just a few years later.

When British Telecommunications was allocated a licence to operate one of two competing cellular networks, provided it entered an equal partnership with a private enterprise, Towle lost no time in suggesting that Securicor fill the gap, a proposal which was welcomed by BT.

Thus, Telecom Securicor Cellular Radio – soon to be called Cellnet – was born. As was often the case, Towle's negotiating skills played a major part in securing an attractive financial deal with BT. His prediction of cellular communications growth, published in the *Financial Times* on March 27th 1985, could not have been more accurate: 'It will start with top management who will think they must have the service. The euphoria will have worn off by the summer and we will be at a second stage, persuading companies that car phones are a cost-effective tool at the middle level. We will be looking at sales and service staff, anyone who has to spend time on the road.'

Having grappled with the immediate problems he faced on joining Securicor, Towle stepped on to the succession ladder when, in 1979, Peter Smith completed his first five years as chairman of both Securicor Group and Security Services, as well as chairman and managing director of Securicor Limited. Reflecting Towle's broader involvement in the affairs of the company than had originally been envisaged, he became director of UK operations, shortly afterwards gaining the post of managing director of Securicor Limited and also being appointed joint managing director (UK) of Securicor International Limited alongside today's group chief executive Roger Wiggs, then responsible for the Group's overseas and legal affairs.

Smith's announcement of his forthcoming retirement in 1985 pushed Towle further up the ladder as he was appointed managing director of Securicor Group plc and Security Services plc, with Wiggs as his deputy. When Smith became non-executive chairman of both Securicor Group and Security Services, Towle was duly appointed group chief executive.

Having sown so many seeds during his progress through the company, Towle's three years at the helm were spent nurturing the new and enlarged businesses. He maintained a relatively low profile, striving always to create firm financial ground in which the managed businesses could thrive and grow.

THE NEW
SECURICOR

4

THE NEW SECURICOR

Roger Wiggs, Group Chief Executive

It was group chief executive Roger Wiggs who manoeuvred Securicor through recession and into the 1990s, positioning its businesses to meet the markets of the new millennium.

As an architect of the 1996 company restructure, which created a single plc in place of two publicly quoted companies, Wiggs has also added credence to the theme of growth through diversification and acquisition which he first expounded when divisionalising group operations at the start of the decade.

Then a useful tactic in surviving recession – businesses with the greatest potential could be quickly identified and that potential maximised, while those which would be damaged by recession could be curtailed or put on hold – divisionalisation has encouraged a concentration of effort on core businesses and the building of sound management structures able to support further innovative development.

Security Services

Henry McKay, Divisional Chief Executive

With the longest history in the Group, Securicor's Security Division is steeped in tradition. While not losing touch with the past, however, it has had to take significant strides since divisionalisation to maintain its reputation as a quality service supplier, major market participant and caring employer.

At the heart of the division are the cash transportation and guarding businesses, the latter of which provided the strength on which Securicor began building its name in the 1930s. These are still key operations, but they have been greatly augmented by both additional service options and entirely new departures such as alarm monitoring and the introduction of custodial services.

Henry McKay, divisional chief executive, has been with the company for 27 years, rising through the ranks from his first job as a cash-in-transit driver. His experience, along with that of his colleagues who manage individual service lines, has been fundamental to grooming and growing an already successful business. Recognising the division's weak spots, identifying emerging markets and consistently meeting customer demands for efficient, effective and reliable services are his external priorities while, within the division, he takes a keen interest in the safety, training and career development of 42,000 employees.

Cash carrying and cash management in the UK, the largest single contributor to the division's 1996 turnover of £417.6 million, is a classic example of Wiggs' diversification theme. Far

■

"We are in the market for today and tomorrow and hence are investing huge amounts of both expertise and technology in our services. Securicor's differentiator is its ability to develop and implement leading-edge technology"

— Henry McKay

■

Serving the retail market

When a company's annual turnover is in excess of £10 billion, the requirement for efficient and secure cash handling is clearly apparent. For over 20 years, Securicor's cash-in-transit fleet has plied between the stores and petrol stations of a leading retailer, collecting cash and cheques for delivery to its bank, as well as transferring money from smaller to larger branches with in-house cash processing facilities.

In addition to providing high-quality day-to-day service, Securicor has built up the relationship to develop new roles. Cash collections and delivery of cheques to banking centres on Sunday have been added, improving the retailer's cash-flow and establishing a round-the-clock, seven-day service.

Working together also enables the customer to tackle potential problems before they materialise and to monitor and review public spending habits with a view to accommodating changes such as the trend towards payment by debit card or cheque rather than cash.

Securicor's cash-in-transit crews are not the only staff working with the retailer. The Security Division also plays a part in providing static guards to secure outlets.

from the fashionable suggestion of a cashless society, Securicor reports that more money than ever is on the move and it has had to develop swiftly to keep up with changing fashions in how customers want that cash to be collected, distributed and managed. Securicor Cash Services, which provides the UK's leading cash collection and delivery service, operates 1,500 secure vehicles and 57 processing centres across the country. Overseas operations bring the fleet to a total of 4,000 vehicles carrying in excess of £1 billion worth of cash and valuables every working day.

While the volume of cash movements has grown consistently, it has not always been easy to benefit from such buoyant conditions, particularly when the market experienced cut-throat pricing as competitors sought to buy market share, an activity in which Securicor chose not to take part. Short-term effects took their toll on profitability as customers voted with their cheque books. But, by holding its ground and its prices, Securicor remained well-placed to pick up customers disgruntled by the soaring costs which accompanied the market's return to a sustainable level.

Indeed, while the main offender found itself in a downward spiral which would lead to its sale to an overseas owner, Securicor could continue to claim a return of 25 per cent on capital employed and 54 per cent of the UK cash-in-transit market when it emerged from the crisis in 1996.

If challenging competition wounded the cash business through the mid-1990s, the battle against bandits added insult to injury. As in the past, however, attacks on both staff and vehicles have brought out the best in Securicor, with technology, processes and procedures evolving to protect staff and customers' valuables from all but the most ruthless and ingenious of crimes.

A spate of attacks on cash handling premises led to the swift installation of extra perimeter protection, while the problem of hostage taking was tackled with new armoured vehicles for the inter-branch network. These no longer provide crew access to the back of the vans, the majority of which are fitted with Datatrak, Securicor's vehicle location and monitoring system, alarms and internal smoke cloak electronic sensors which are activated should a perpetrator attempt to cut into the sides of the vehicle body.

On a less dramatic, but equally vital, note, an investment of over £6 million in a fully automated tracking and tracing system will enable Securicor to identify each individual container and its movement, as well as giving customers online access to information about their consignments – a first in the UK market and an important step towards meeting growing demand for real-time management information.

Innovation has also played its part as the division's Cash Services operation has responded to the changing requirements of its traditional banking, building society and large retail customers, as well as tapping into new markets. Finding itself with an excess of staff and processing facilities as demand for wage packeting dwindled in the early 1980s, the division set up a specialist banking support operation in 1982. Handling over £30 billion a year, it covers a range of cash counting and distribution services, as well as overseeing the burgeoning business of automated teller machine replenishment and maintenance.

A leader in the UK ATM replenishment and first-line maintenance business, Cash Services is also exporting its skills to less developed banking markets. The Far East was the first stop on the map, but similar provision will be made in Central America and Africa as the division benefits from its presence in over 40 territories across the world and adds to the 10,000 ATMs it attends every day.

In the early 1990s, the business played a key role in combating credit card intercept fraud through a collection and distribution system to ensure personal delivery of credit cards to consumers in high risk security areas. Among its first customers, one major bank achieved savings of £5 million a year as a result of using the service at that time.

At the other end of the spectrum, new opportunities have been identified in small businesses. The division's Business-Link service, initially launched under the Cash Guard brand, runs a fleet of compact, secure vehicles designed for those wishing to move smaller amounts of money, supporting cash transit with

■

"The way I look at it as far as bandits are concerned is that we are in the war and are determined to win. We will lose some battles, but we will win the war"

– Henry McKay

■

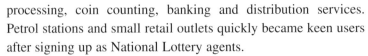

processing, coin counting, banking and distribution services. Petrol stations and small retail outlets quickly became keen users after signing up as National Lottery agents.

Cash Services continues to research and develop new technologies to not only increase efficiency, but also to cut customers' costs through both direct savings and increasingly secure cash handling processes. In place of the predominantly manual systems used to count the huge volumes of cash which Securicor collects and counts on behalf of its banking and commercial customers, a factory processing style system using automated equipment was trialled to count and sort money. When completed, the potential step-change from manual to automated systems will provide dramatic benefits.

"Through the development of our staff we can offer a total package of top-quality integrated services to customers worldwide, at the same time giving a good return to all stakeholders in the company"

– Henry McKay

Following a few years of both UK and overseas expansion, the latter primarily through acquisition, McKay envisages a period of consolidation across Cash Services as he seeks consistent profitability, coupled with stable cash-flow, in a business which has grown exponentially since its inception.

Like the division's cash carrying and management services, Securicor Guarding has a long and distinguished history, remaining one of the Group's core business interests to this day. But, like its sibling, it has had to refuse the temptation of living on past success and recognise the need to change with the times, generating new services to match customer demands as well as keeping pace with developments in technology.

Divisionalisation in 1989 gave Guarding its own identity, with dedicated management and sales teams, which quickly led to a UK turnover of £50 million a year. The 1995 acquisition of Shorrock Guards proved the biggest fillip in the operation's recent history, however, bringing the total UK guarding force to over 7,000 and quadrupling manned guarding profits in the 1996 financial year.

The guarding service also features strongly in each of the division's four overseas geographical areas, which cover Europe and the Middle East, Asia Pacific, Africa and the Americas. Some 35,000 guards are employed worldwide and it is their careful selection and training which is key to business success.

Across the Group, Securicor has always been proud of both the ability and integrity of its staff, promising its employees career development prospects and its customers hand-picked workers.

The division's policy of checking potential recruits' employment and personal records as far back as 20 years was necessarily time consuming and this affected its ability to recruit quickly. Working with an occupational psychologist, the division developed a battery of psychometric tests covering an applicant's honesty, reliability and temperament, with the result that it can confidently offer employment on a temporary basis within hours while the necessary references were sought. This enabled the division to steal a march on competitors working exclusively with employment records.

Besides supplying traditional markets in commerce and industry with services ranging from key-holding and patrols to full-time guards and sophisticated surveillance centres, Securicor Guarding has expanded into niche markets. Particularly notable are its successes in ensuring safety and security at party political conferences and other major public events, as well as its work at UK and international airports and ports, and its presence at sporting events – all contributors to the public image which Securicor holds so dear.

Remembering the dual methods of growth espoused by Roger Wiggs, the Security Division has achieved significant organic growth in its long-established cash and guarding businesses, but it has also diversified through acquisition and keeping a sharp eye on the markets in which it works.

Securicor Alarms provides a case in point. A late developer under the auspices of Peter Towle, the business picked up following the acquisition of a range of well-respected products but soon hit a flat market, leaving McKay to question its future. Considering both trends in buying patterns and the role of the police in serving the public, he exchanged Securicor's alarms business for Shorrock's guarding operation and in its place created an alarm monitoring service which would build on Securicor's communications skills and provide a service better aligned to the changing law enforcement environment.

Banking on Securicor

Working with the Cash Services operation of the Security Division for over 10 years, a major high-street bank has built a strong yet flexible business partnership with Securicor. Besides using the company's cash-in-transit fleet to carry money to and from its 2,000 nationwide branches, the bank uses Securicor for collecting cash from its customers and processing it for bulk delivery to a cash centre. The reverse sequence – making up cash consignments on behalf of the bank for delivery to customers – is also part of the package.

The bank believes Securicor's established infrastructure and, most importantly, its nationwide overnight trunking network make it the most appropriate partner in the market able to deliver a cost-effective service to branches and customers.

Beyond cash collection and distribution, Securicor also works with other banking operations to replenish and service automated teller machines, as well as handling foreign notes and coins.

Building a partnership

Having developed a long-standing relationship with Securicor, one London-based friendly society contracts a regular team of guards from the company, including them in its overall security plan.

Nine regular guards man its office premises during the day, with four covering the night shift and three holding the fort at the weekend. From a central control room equipped with closed-circuit television, alarms and monitors, the guards keep an eye on the comings and goings of visitors to the building, as well as covering its four entrances, making regular patrols and logging day-to-day incidents with a view to briefing the following guarding team.

The society praises Securicor Guarding for never letting it down and always responding to problems quickly. On a more personal note, it describes the Securicor guards as diligent and well-presented.

Acquisitions were made in Germany, Switzerland and France, a new business was set up in Africa and Securicor reaped the rewards of its reputation in the swift market acceptance of Monitoring Services. In Europe and Africa, where the police have relinquished their responsibility for providing a first response to alarm calls, business is burgeoning, while McKay forecasts a similar change in UK police duties within the next few years, resulting in a major home market.

Offering dual command and control centres servicing every region in which it operates, Securicor is poised for success. Meantime it maintains the middle ground in the UK, with a staff of about 18,000 working around the clock to respond to alarm calls and notify keyholders and police. Customers come from its industrial base, but it is also dipping into other divisions' specialisms, particularly the emergency services which are already users of the Communications Division's vehicle track and trace systems.

Diversification to embrace and make best use of change is nowhere more evident than in the division's Custodial Services operation, set up in 1990 in response to a government decision to contract out selected prisoner services. Already the winner of the largest contract in Security Services' history – a five-year commitment to operate the London Metropolitan Court Escort and Custody service – the business unit has enormous potential.

Based on the principles of security, reliability and integrity, the operation benefits both from the Group's long-term experience and more recent developments. While secure vehicles and the Datatrak track and trace system play their part, so too do new-found technological skills, which earned Custodial Services a contract to pilot electronic monitoring of offenders.

Under the stewardship of managing director Richard Powell, Custodial Services currently employs 1,300 people and operates 150 custom-built vehicles, numbers which are guaranteed to grow substantially as more contracts for prisoner escort services are put out to tender and governments both in the UK and overseas turn to the security industry to design, build, finance and manage new prisons.

In the UK, a consortium including Securicor Custodial Services is responsible for the construction and operation of an 800-bed prison at Bridgend, South Wales. Due to open in late 1997, it will be among the most technologically advanced establishments in the world and is one of the government's first private finance initiative contracts, running a length of 25 years.

With its core businesses clearly defined, management structures in place and growth plans in progress, Security Services has become a highly integrated operation, building on its internal experience but also that of its co-divisions to maximise market potential.

On the premises

When a major motor dealership began to suffer an intolerable level of theft and vandalism at its premises, it was time to bring in the security experts.

A portacabin was erected on the seven-acre site, a telephone installed and Securicor guards recruited to cover both night and Sunday shifts, patrolling both the exterior of the showrooms and offices, and also providing support to the company's forecourt staff who work throughout the night.

The two regular guards on patrol visit 11 bar-coded points around the site every hour and then upload the log to a central system which later produces a monthly report of all location visits. The on-duty guard is also connected by radio to forecourt staff to ensure their security, while a radio link to the local Securicor supervisor provides additional back-up should assistance be required.

With millions of pounds worth of new and used cars on the premises, the customer reports that no cars have been stolen out of business hours, nor any vehicles vandalised, since the night the first Securicor guard arrived. Taking on a security firm may initially have appeared expensive, but Securicor's excellent record has meant a reduction in insurance costs and less sleepless nights for the company's executives.

Security Division growth

	Turnover (£m)	Pre-tax profit (£m)
1992	274.1	5.6
1993	285.2	9.1
1994	307.7	12.0
1995	359.6	13.1*
1996	417.6	12.0*

*Profit before interest and taxation

■

"I've done everything from driving a cash-in-transit vehicle to working in accounting and personnel. Now my job is as a support service, opening doors and giving regional and business directors the tools to help them do their jobs"

– Henry McKay

■

SECURITY SERVICES: THE PEOPLE

A veteran of Securicor's cash carrying team, **Doug Bradley** joined the company in 1964 as a cash-in-transit driver based in South London. He moved to the busy Nine Elms depot in the mid-1980s and has since worked on transporting coins between customer premises and Securicor's cash processing centres.

While much of his time is spent working with financial institutions in the City of London, Doug does have occasion to venture further afield in his 16-ton armoured truck and also takes a part in managing the stores and transport back at base.

"The coin bags weigh about 20 lbs each – at first they seemed heavy, but after 32 years you don't notice how many you carry back and forth every day. Having been in the job a long time I'm pretty well known on the cash-in-transit runs and I enjoy meeting the customers," he says.

Doug has been the subject of seven criminal attacks during his career with Securicor Cash Services, but rather than undermining his confidence, he believes such incidents have added to his experience, making him increasingly aware of problems which may occur and alerting him and other drivers to the potential dangers of cash carrying.

If you don't know **Chris Stebbing**'s mobile phone number, you don't know Chris Stebbing. As Securicor Guarding's City of London regional manager, Chris spends the majority of his time out and about, visiting major financial customers in the Square Mile as well as the guards who man their premises.

After 13 years in the Coldstream Guards, Chris joined the security business and was working with Shorrock Guards when it merged with Securicor Guarding in April 1996.

"The takeover gave me a bigger area to cover and obviously there was a change in procedures such as paperwork, but we've got to grips with that. As part of the Securicor Group, I feel there are opportunities not only for promotion within guarding but also to other operations in the Security Division.' he says.

The working day can be long and Chris is on call around the clock. But it is a price he is prepared to pay for a flexible, enjoyable and challenging job which, behind the frontline of customer and staff communication, includes selecting and placing guards, budgeting and, above all, quality control.

Joe Dowd, divisional transport manager with the Security Division, has had a long and varied career within the Group. Joining in 1968 as a vehicle inspector at a cash-in-transit base in Liverpool, he quickly progressed to take on regional and divisional responsibility for the North of England and Northern Ireland, before being despatched to Nairobi for a four-year stint managing the company's transport investments in Kenya, Malawi and Zambia.

On his return in 1985, he became assistant national transport manager within Securicor Vehicle Services, before being promoted to technical manager and moving on to his current post at Security Services in 1993.

"I have responsibility for divisional transport and transport management around the world and also support the design and building of new vehicles. I suspect I also have one of the biggest phone bills in the company!" he says.

When not on the telephone, Joe is likely to be found travelling abroad, talking to the staff who drive the fleet, the committee which works on vehicle design and the managers who must plan for both today's and tomorrow's transport requirements. With armoured vans costing anything up to £80,000 each, Joe's phone bill is only a drop in the ocean of the Security Division's investment in a first-class vehicle fleet.

As a national accounts manager in the Security Division, **Ray Jacobs** works with the UK's leading retail banks and building societies, developing business partnerships to support existing needs for cash services as well as working with customers to project future market trends. After nearly two decades with the security division, he is well-versed on its portfolio and uses his knowledge to match customer requests to service offerings across the business as well as to tackle problems.

'I left school wanting to be either a policeman or a salesman. I wasn't tall enough to be a policeman, but have thoroughly

■

"Overseas business is a key contributor to Security Services and with further expansion will generate about half our profits by the year 2000. That is not to say UK growth is unimportant, but close analysis did lead me to conclude that if Securicor was to be a major global player, it needed to put in local management resources. We now have five regions spanning the world, each with their own managing director. In 1989 we operated in 19 territories, now we cover 35 and all the regions are developing"
– Henry McKay

■

enjoyed my career in sales. No two days are the same and no two opportunities are alike. Working in national accounts adds to the responsibility and importance attached to the job – the five accounts I look after represent about 18 per cent of the total cash-in-transit turnover," he says.

New opportunities for Jacobs include the potential of stronger customer relations through the implementation of Securicor's developing information systems, which not only improve efficiency, but, from a sales and marketing point of view, enhance the management information needed to offer customers a proactive service.

Accounting for well over a third of Group turnover in 1996, with revenues of £470 million and a 50 per cent profit gain to £21 million, Securicor Distribution has grown consistently since the early days of divisionalisation. Not content to be a parochial parcels distributor working predominantly in the UK market, it has followed a policy of acquisition and diversification to shed its label as a parcels carrier and ensure its position on the international stage as a multi-disciplined distribution and logistics operation.

Recognising customers' ever increasing needs to improve the supply chain, it is now as well placed to deliver a manila envelope to Malaysia as a pallet of industrial goods from Birmingham to Belgium, to pick and pack warehoused products for retail distribution or transport containers for the world's shipping lines.

While Peter Towle was key to the early development of the parcels division, its repositioning as Securicor Distribution and recent success must be attributed to chief executive Pat Howes. Like so many of Securicor's top managers, he has worked his way up through the company.

After joining the security operation as a patrolman based at the Norwich branch in 1969, Howes soon became a supervisor of both static guards and patrolmen, before being elevated to branch manager in 1970. The job of zone manager was quick to follow and, with the reorganisation of the group into regions in 1974, Howes was appointed Eastern regional manager before becoming Midlands area manager in a 1982 restructure which saw the Group redefined as five trading operations – including the Freight and Parcels Division – working across three regions.

The birth of the parcels division, however, was to change Howes' career path. In 1983 he moved to London as general manager of the UK operation, joining the board of Securicor Ltd in 1986 and becoming parcels divisional chief executive in 1989. He took his seat on the main group board in 1992.

From its early days as a parcels carrier, the division's profitable growth has been based, in part, on an intimate knowledge of its customers and an ability to spot and fill gaps in the market. Equally important has been recognition of the value of employees, who now number over 10,000.

Distribution

Pat Howes, Securicor Distribution's Chief Executive

■

"It's very important to spend a lot of time with customers. Personally, I think it is a key aspect of my job: listening to customers, meeting their needs and considering future requirements"

– Pat Howes

■

It all started as something of an *ad hoc* affair, however, built on Securicor's reputation in the security market. In the mid-1960s, the company began to carry data between its retail banking customers in a few Ford Zephyr cars and Securicor Data Services was born. Before long it started taking in the odd parcel, quickly expanding beyond the banking sector and moving forward in leaps and bounds when a Post Office strike in the early 1970s left businesses across the country looking for alternative carriers. By 1983 it could claim an annual turnover of more than £60 million worth of UK business.

The creation of the parcels division as a separate business unit in 1989 proved a significant factor in generating today's diversified operation. At that stage, the business was focused almost exclusively on the UK, with European operations and the Pony Express same-day courier service as second strings.

■

"Customers know they can count on us for reliability, quality of service, smartly turned out staff, liveried vehicles, effective tracking and tracing systems and, ultimately, efficient billing systems"

– Pat Howes

■

Howes' first initiative was to create a divisional board to oversee development and secure strong management teams for each operation. With a central core in place and Securicor Parcels already the UK's largest overnight carrier in the business-to-business sector, he then set about the dual tasks of giving the UK business its own distinctive identity and developing a pan-European service. While the former was an unqualified success, with the launch of the Securicor Omega Express brand in 1990, the latter proved more tortuous.

An initial network based on small Securicor branches in a number of Continental European countries foundered, unable to compete with entrenched local carriers. Similarly, an early attempt at carrying freight into Europe using a specially purchased aircraft never lived up to expectations. With the prospect of European unity just over the horizon, Securicor needed to completely rethink its involvement or face the slow, painful demise of its lack-lustre European subsidiaries.

Never one to give up, Howes called on his team and the wide experience in Europe of chief executive Roger Wiggs to rewrite the business plan. Local domestic units would be run down or sold while, at the same time, an international operations team would be built to develop a European network based on 48- and 72-hour road services. In place of Securicor-owned local operations, exclusive business agreements with partners in western Europe and Scandinavia would provide mutual collection and delivery services.

The decision to rethink the business plan was bold, but it proved propitious. In 1992 Securicor Network Europe was launched, providing a template for European growth. Noting growing demand for multi-modal distribution and customers' desires to simplify their own operations through one-stop shopping, in 1993 Securicor took the acquisition trail to buy Scottish Express International, adding international air and sea freight, plus European heavyweight distribution, to its service portfolio.

At a total cost of around £4 million, Scottish Express International was acquired at asset value and, more importantly as a foothold to the future, immediately added about £20 million worth of European and international distribution and air and sea freight business to the division, along with a number of new and prestigious customer names such as computer suppliers IBM and Digital.

Back at home, the UK parcels distribution operation under the Securicor Omega Express brand was achieving strong organic growth but also making major moves which would allow substantial change. 1992 provided the opportunity to purchase Federal Express's UK domestic customer base and seal a deal with the US carrier to distribute and collect from international Fed Ex customers outside the boundary of the M25 motorway.

The acquisition of Pony Express back in 1981 was no less fortuitous. It was quickly turned from a loss-making, door-to-door service for small parcels and documents working only in London

■

"At the end of the day we want to give customers a total service, from delivering raw materials to storing, picking and packing, and distributing products. We are also working to reverse the logistics chain, taking products and packaging at the end of their life for recycling"

– Pat Howes

■

to a nationally operating profit contributor. Adding same-day courier services to the division's range, it has secured long-term contracts with Securicor customers old and new. A country-wide franchise scheme is spreading the net, making the livery of Securicor Pony Express bike riders as familiar in towns and cities across the country as Omega Express vans have become in the high street.

The change from parcels carrier to full-service logistics supplier followed the £50 million acquisition of Russell Davies in 1995. Securicor's largest investment to date, it heralded a name change from Securicor Parcels to Securicor Distribution and the bringing together of individual business lines into a cohesive matrix able to market a comprehensive range of warehousing, distribution and freight services.

Little known under its Russell Davies Distribution banner, the distribution business was rebranded Securicor Omega Logistics and, with all the connotations of being part of a large and respected company, had an immediate impact on the market.

A potential gem, Securicor Omega Logistics arrived at exactly the right moment to take advantage of a customer base shifting its commitment to core product processing and manufacture while looking to external suppliers to service the supply chain. In a competitive economy where every penny counts, however, chosen suppliers must be able to adapt to changing demand and consider the cost efficiencies which they can offer to customers. It is here that Securicor Omega Logistics excels. With no hard and fast traditions, the business shone as it responded to customer demands. Shared-user warehousing, by way of example, allows customers to pay for warehouse and

■

"Working for Securicor becomes more than a job – it's a way of life. Drivers wear a uniform and feel part of the company, long-service and loyalty are recognised at frequent awards ceremonies and over 50 staff have made it to the One Million Milers Club, a journey which takes about 15 years"

– Pat Howes

■

vehicle space as and when they need it, avoiding the costs of pre-buying space which they may or may not use. Further down the supply chain, the company is working with major food retailers to eliminate wasted journeys by running full loads in and out of regional distribution centres.

If Russell Davies Distribution was a little-known, yet emerging, quantity, Russell Davies Container Transport needed no introduction following the takeover by Securicor Distribution. As UK market leader, the company handled over 1,500 containers a day for many of the world's largest ocean carriers.

Headquartered in Ipswich, the company has a presence at most of the UK's major ports and in 1996 invested £2.5 million in enhanced container depot facilities at its Felixstowe site, as well as significant sums elsewhere as it bought land and buildings, installed sophisticated container handling equipment and continued to develop its IT-based container transport management system.

Despite, or perhaps because of, his length of service with Securicor, divisional chief executive Pat Howes is an enthusiast for new technology, believing that business cannot be won without it and that it is fundamental in distinguishing Distribution's services from the crowd.

Securicor Omega Express, the division's largest component, is the beneficiary of the highest IT investment with a multi-million pound annual budget for both new systems and day-to-day operations. Key to the business are the

Capacity planning

A global supplier with over 60,000 product lines ranging from stationery and surgical supplies to laser imaging and x-ray machines chose Securicor Omega Express to deliver over 350,000 parcels a year to UK outlets. Keeping tabs on such a huge number of product movements is helped by the supplier's adoption of Omega Trans.IT and a link to the Signline proof-of-delivery system.

Besides carrying goods from the company's manufacturing sites to its distribution centre, Omega Express also makes daily journeys to thousands of customers around the UK, delivering to corner shops, retail chains, hospitals and businesses.

The customer reports that close to 100 per cent of orders arrive next day using Omega's overnight services for parcels up to 25kg in weight, while the two-to-three-day service provides carriage for goods up to 50kg. The full breadth of Securicor's distribution expertise is utilised, with palletised loads for the UK being carried by Scottish Express International, while Omega Express's European network handles parcels destined for the continent.

Designs on delivery

Expertise in carrying bulky items won Securicor Omega Express the distribution business of a well-known fabric and wallpaper supplier, which involves handling over 150,000 parcels per year. Since the early 1980s, Omega Express has been carrying its products to 3,000 UK outlets on both next-day and two-to-three-day schedules. Picking up wallpaper and fabric from a base in west London, and collecting packaged goods such as linen and ready-made curtains from Lancashire Securicor's blue vans deliver both to major retailers' central warehouses and direct to high-street stores.

The supplier prides itself on a quick turnaround, with urgent orders received in the morning despatched the same evening and delivered next day. Omega Express matches the company's customer service standards and provides reliable distribution at a competitive cost. Frequent reviews of available carriers consistently put Omega Express at the top of the supplier's distributor list, although it has turned to a small dedicated carrier to handle its paint products after packaging and handling problems left Omega Express with a number of internally redecorated vans and paint daubed depots!

Signline proof of delivery system, the Omegaline collection request facility and Trans.IT, the customer-based despatch and management system.

A pioneer in information systems, Omega Express has long been a user of barcode labels to track and trace parcels, but is no stranger to emerging technologies such as electronic data interchange, voice recognition and radio frequency communication, which have all been adopted.

Technology is certainly to the fore at a distribution centre being developed at Hatfield, Hertfordshire. Costing £30 million and due to open in 1997, the centre is among the most advanced in the world and is installed with handling equipment which will ultimately process up to 36,000 parcels an hour, leaving the door open for Securicor Omega Express to increase the two million parcels it collects, sorts and distributes on a weekly basis.

Branch staff are also being equipped with leading-edge technology, including sorting equipment which generates barcoded routeing labels in response to spoken operator instructions and hand-held terminals which allow drivers to relay delivery information directly to a central computer system, updating customer records and presenting the latter with a clear and instant picture of the location of their consignments.

As Howes points out, while companies entrust the physical carriage of goods to third parties, their need for accurate and timely management information escalates as, in turn, they endeavour to provide their customers with top-quality services. Such customer-led demand is further reflected in the services which Omega Express offers through its nationwide network of 100 branches, 8,500 staff and fleet of over 4,000 vehicles. An appraisal of timed delivery options, for example, highlighted the need for Omega Diamond, an overnight service which guarantees delivery by 10.00am next morning. While customers can choose from a range of schedules, including next-day and economy two-day delivery, Diamond is our first UK service to guarantee arrival and promise financial compensation for failure – recognition of a market driven by the need for speed and efficiency, but also an indication of Omega Express's confidence in its own ability.

Elsewhere, Securicor Omega Express International and Scottish Express International are also maturing, building distribution networks with partners across the European Continent and around the world, both supported by extensive internal IT systems and also SEI's membership of the independent Hi-Tech Forwarder Network, which allows air and sea freight customers to pin-point a consignment at any stage of its journey.

Expansion of volume and the service portfolio is also being catered for with Scottish Express International's opening of a purpose-built international freight depot at the Eurotunnel railhead at Mossend in Glasgow and Omega Express's branch re-engineering programme.

The necessary investment runs to many millions of pounds, but management can be safe in the knowledge that it has gained the critical mass which will generate further development and, equally important, provide a springboard for new adventures.

Among those already trialled are the business-to-business postal service which was successfully conducted during Post Office disputes in 1996 and could swing into action should the government choose to end the Post Office monopoly. Also under consideration are reverse logistics, which will be needed as companies meet the Environmental Agency deadline for recycling waste and packaging.

While these may be lofty aspirations, at the other end of the scale is the fledgling office services business, which includes mailroom management, archiving and shredding, while the idea of using a Rolls Royce confiscated after a gang robbery perpetrated against Cash Services led to the development of a fleet of chauffeur-driven executive cars.

So too are small overseas operations – once run within the confines of locally established Securicor security businesses – being developed as entities in their own right, with dedicated management and enhancement strategies.

The sum of the many constituents which comprise Securicor Distribution is a credit to Howes and the management team he is building to take the business into the 21st century. Each service may seem minor in relation to the scale of many customers, but all

Hatfield – close to a quarter of a mile in length

■

"Technology is vitally important and puts us a step ahead of our competitors. It also locks in customers by making them an integral part of our information network. We practise what we preach, encouraging customers to join us in business partnerships and adding credence to the philosophy that together we can both grow profitably"

– Pat Howes

■

are carefully considered milestones along the route to fulfilling market demand for competent and cost-effective distribution and logistics services throughout the supply chain.

Distribution Division growth

	Turnover (£m)	Pre-tax profit (£m)
1992	224.9	4.6
1993	241.1	5.7
1994	312.5	9.9
1995	380.4	13.4*
1996	470.0	21.0*

*Profit before interest and taxation

DISTRIBUTION SERVICES: THE PEOPLE

Having been a member of the Group for 30 years, **Richard Benson** is typical of the young men and women who joined Securicor in its formative years and have since climbed to management positions. Starting his career at 22 as part-time guard number 959 at Cadbury Schweppes in south east London, a full-time guarding post soon followed before Benson was asked to move to the control room at Swan House. In the days when refusal to do as asked all too frequently resulted in a foreshortened career, Benson headed for Chelsea and the job of control room sergeant.

Like so many, Benson's career made an abrupt about turn when he was despatched by Keith Erskine to run newly-acquired Janitorial Services, a cleaning company which included Buckingham Palace among its customers. Having been marked out by Erskine as a man manager, Benson had previously enjoyed a number of jobs, including a stint in the diamond fields of Sierra Leone and a secondment to look after reclusive millionaire Howard Hughes.

After pitching about in the ever-changing seas of Securicor's security services, Benson found his niche as managing director of the Pony Express courier company and, by 1989, he was running a £10 million company and orchestrating a merger with another member of the Group, Auto Parts Express. The result was Securicor Pony Express, a streamlined operation handling £20 million worth of business a year.

Divisionalisation of the Group at the turn of the 1990s opened the next door and Benson was soon installed in Sutton as managing director of Securicor Parcels Service, now operating under the Securicor Omega Express brand.

Would he do it all again?

"Yes, most definitely. In over 30 years I've always enjoyed coming to work. It's so diverse and I have worked with so many interesting people. The high incidence of long service is a reflection of the company's style and the way most senior people have come up through the company. Even now, if staff stay for six months they're likely to stay a lot longer – Securicor staff are like sticks of seaside rock: cut them in half and they say Securicor all the way through."

A drive from Aberdeen to Bracknell – and back again – is all part of a week's work for **Gavin Crane**, a Securicor Omega Logistics employee based in Norwich. Primarily transporting Britvic products around the country, Gavin drives a 38-ton articulated lorry with a 45-foot trailer.

"I enjoy getting about and seeing different places and the staff at Norwich are a good crowd. The lorry is equipped with a portable phone so I am in touch and can sometimes meet up with other drivers. I might be away from home and the family all week, but I'm always home at the weekend."

Having been with the company for over 10 years, Gavin recalls the 1995 takeover of Russell Davies by Securicor. He reports no adverse effects on his job and only the pride of being among the first drivers to be allocated a lorry carrying the new Securicor Omega Logistics livery.

Peter Bennett, deputy general manager of Russell Davies Container Transport, another 10-year veteran, joined from the

Old friends

One of the high street banks was among the first to sign up following the launch of Data Transit Services in the mid-1960s. The relationship has endured, evolving to meet the increasingly competitive and commercial nature of the banking industry.

The bank's 800 branches are visited by Securicor Omega Express every week-day evening, with 16 tons of documents collected and returned to headquarters in central London for sorting and redirection. Double the quantity is returned by a fleet of Omega Express vehicles working through the night to reach branches by 9am next morning. This service is augmented by Securicor Pony Express, which provides a range of same-day delivery services.

Accidents are inevitable in such a long business partnership, but the bank reports few incidents and only positive assistance when things go wrong. For example, when an Omega Express van full of bank documents spontaneously burst into flames, a Securicor executive immediately organised for the van to be returned to a nearby branch and accommodated bank staff while they carefully salvaged whatever they could from the burnt out shell, thereby helping the bank to keep losses to a minimum.

A critical link in the supply chain

From its purpose-built warehousing and distribution complex, an electronic component supplier fills and despatches orders to consumer electronics concerns across the country, priding itself on next-day delivery of all orders made before its 5.30pm closing time. Working in partnership, Securicor Omega Express plays a key role in this service, making three calls to the supplier's site every day to collect barcoded parcels over 1kg. These are taken to SOE's local branch before being transferred to a regional terminal for sorting and overnight distribution.

Omega Express's consistently high level of service at an attractive price has drawn praise from the company, as have the friendly and efficient Securicor staff, who are commended for their willingness to tackle and resolve potential problems.

The company is already using SOE's Signline proof-of-delivery system for faxed confirmation of delivery to pass on to its customers and hopes to add another layer of quality to its customer service through full implementation of an acknowledgement of receipt system based on electronic data interchange technology.

shipping side of the transport industry and has first-hand knowledge of customer needs. Today, he works with two major customers, importing and exporting thousands of containers a year, as well as collecting and distributing their contents around the UK.

"I spend much of my time dealing with customers, developing our relationships and working with them to overcome problems – that's where the real satisfaction lies."

As a member of the Russell Davies team when Securicor acquired the company, Peter believes the firm has managed to maintain its family feeling while gaining the advantages of belonging to a large group.

Roger Capper joined Securicor Omega Express soon after leaving university, following the company's one-year management training scheme and, at the age of just 27, was rewarded with the job of Kingston branch manager. Responsible for 65 staff and 38 vehicles, Roger makes customer service a top priority.

"The unpredictability of every day is what makes the job so interesting. One day we may handle 3,000 parcels, the next 4,500. When I arrive at the branch in the morning I never know what will happen – that's the challenge."

Like so many before him, Roger's early years with the Group gave him an insight into the career ladder ahead and he is keen to start climbing, perhaps with a move to a larger branch or to manage a regional terminal.

Having worked as a Securicor Omega Express driver for over three years, **Mark McLean** was promoted to a supervisor's post at the Coventry branch. With 120 staff, parcel volumes of around 6,500 a day and 50 vehicles based at the site, there is always plenty to be done, from customer liaison to sorting out individual driver's concerns.

Working the 1.30pm to 10pm shift, Mark is briefed by the early shift supervisors before tackling work in progress.

"It's madly busy here every morning and every evening so there is great satisfaction in making sure everything gets sorted out by the end of the day."

His next move, on completion of the supervisor's development programme, could be to an assistant manager's position, a prospect he looks forward to in a company which offers both career progress and job security.

As credit control manager of Securicor Omega Express, **Mick Roberts** is responsible for collecting all the money owed by customers to the business. Having joined the company in January 1968, he has built his career in credit control, with the exception of a six-month exile in 1973 when he was consigned to sales following a disagreement with then chairman and managing director Keith Erskine.

"We can be owed up to £40 million at any one time, but we have minimal bad debts. My job is to lead the team which checks credit, implement board policy on financial arrangements and keep up with the work being done at our four offices around the country. I also work closely with credit control departments in other Securicor companies as we try to make each other aware of potential problems."

With many years of service already notched up, Mick remembers the days when all staff were obliged to do at least two days of cash-in-transit work a week, as well as fill unforeseen gaps on the guarding roster. This did nothing to put him off, however, and he remains of the opinion that a job with Securicor offers a variety of work in a challenging and growing environment hard to find elsewhere.

Geoff Laidlaw applied for a job as a security patrolman in 1968, but realised at interview that the job was not for him. Instead he suggested joining the Group's data service as a courier. In those early days of the distribution business, much work needed to be done and Geoff was swiftly promoted to become the manager of the central Brixton branch in South London.

A stint developing the European distribution network was followed by the task of setting up a planning department for the UK trunk network and later promotion to a seat on the operational board set up by chief executive of the time, Peter Towle. Despite

Motoring forward

In the heart of rural mid-Wales, a supplier of variable speed drives for incorporation in equipment as diverse as jogging machines and oil rig drills is forging an international business.

Working on a just-in-time production basis, the company ships products every day through its distribution partner, Scottish Express International. With outgoing parcels weighing from 5kg to 120kg and destined for locations across Europe and the Asia-Pacific region, the supplier was looking for a large yet flexible carrier when it moved its manufacturing premises in the early 1990s.

The manufacturer commends the flexibility which Scottish Express International offers as a global service provider and, closer to home, is realising the benefits of an IT hook-up to Coalville, allowing it to book transport directly, label freight and monitor consignments' delivery status. Scottish Express International's leading role in the worldwide Hi-Tech Forwarder Network will also provide business benefits as the Tracknet database develops to give online access to proof of delivery data.

Swift and sure

After rethinking its parts distribution service in 1992, a major information systems supplier now relies on Pony Express to both hold parts and deliver them to engineers working on site within the timescales needed to meet service contracts, which often demand computer repair within as little as two hours.

From a standing start, Pony Express has developed five parts banks spanning the UK from Vauxhall in London to Leeds, Manchester, Newcastle and Glasgow. Each holds about 200 different items, ranging from a personal computer mouse to a replacement part for an automated teller machine. A request from the supplier's customer service centre is immediately acknowledged and the necessary part couriered to the named site, while confirmation of shipment to the supplier's stock system automatically reorders product for delivery to the Pony Express parts bank.

Electronic links between the customer service centre and the parts banks have been developed to further increase efficiency, while the information systems expert also notes improvements in stock control and its ability to meet contractual commitments as a result of the scheme.

having little practical experience, Geoff was charged with responsibility for materials handling. He took up the ball and has continued to run with it, his now ample experience warranting the title of health, safety and handling manager for the division.

'My job has grown consistently as the volume of traffic has increased. I've selected locations and equipped sites, set up depots and trunking systems. I constantly review new equipment and make recommendations for improvement, as well as keeping up a maintenance and replacement programme.'

Securicor certainly wasn't Geoff's initial dream. He left home at 12 to become an apprentice jockey and only joined the commercial world when he couldn't afford to pay his mortgage.

Communications

Unlike its counterparts in security and parcels, Securicor Communications is a relative newcomer as a division in its own right and has very different characteristics to the longer established services.

Depending on technology investment and development rather than large numbers of people, the division's staff numbers are comparatively low. It is as likely to be found marketing its wares in New York as it is in Newcastle and it has, in chief executive Ed Hough, a leader with commercial experience gained outside the Securicor fold.

Hough's mission is clearly stated: to make the Communications Division as important to the Group as security and distribution by the year 2000. There is some way to go to meet this goal, but, like many Securicor businesses in the past, Communications has much to draw on from within the Group as well as an active acquisition plan.

Early experience in both private mobile radio and vehicle tracking for internal use has proved invaluable in creating marketable products and services while, in the early 1980s, chief executive Peter Towle's interest in communications gave Securicor an opening into the burgeoning cellular market and the foresight to join BT in developing the Cellnet cellular telephone network.

When Communications was recognised as one of five key divisions in the 1989 reorganisation, however, its operations were fragmented. Pockets of expertise dotted about the Group predominantly supported internal Securicor operations, while external customer-facing businesses were dominated by the sale of cellular telephones and telephony systems. In 1991, the division recorded turnover of about £30 million, but was losing over £10 million.

When Ed Hough was brought in as chief executive in 1992, the winds of change began to blow. He set about an audit of the division's activities, then, with a view to commercial rather than technical development, rebuilt the division to include key business areas under the Securicor Communications holding company name. Each would have its own management, responsible for development plans and financial returns.

Ed Hough, Chief Executive of Securicor Communications

"My focus is on turning a technically-driven collection of services, initially developed for in-house use, into a broad portfolio of commercial communications companies operating in international markets"

– Ed Hough

These businesses have earned Securicor a place in the fast-moving telecommunications market as a full-service provider, from network supply, through systems integration, network operation and, ultimately, service provision.

Starting at the top of the value chain, Securicor Cellular Services, a cellphone and airtime provider set up independently of Securicor's involvement in Cellnet to comply with government restrictions on network operators, currently accounts for a major share of the division's total turnover. By 1996 it had connected almost 400,000 subscribers to the Cellnet network, was turning over £200 million a year and continuing to find market potential for equipment and services sold both through its own sales force and selected high street dealers.

While the market proved active in 1996, it was a year of belt-tightening as Securicor and its competitors were beset by the problems of a shift in subscribers from the business to the consumer sector and the high level of bad debt in the latter. Having written off the debt and taken precautions to minimise future risk, the business is well placed to profit from a strong subscriber base and continuing market demand for mobile communications.

While Securicor's success in cellular communications owes much to far-sighted decision making in the early 1980s, other businesses in services provision have their roots in more recent internal developments. Building on its work in both vehicle tracking and mobile communications, the division's TrakBak stolen vehicle recovery system, which, as a theft attempt is made, alerts a control centre which is then able to guide police to the vehicle, last year signed up its 6,000th subscriber and is moving consistently towards profitability.

SecurIT, once the Group's internal information systems provider, has also developed a market profile and is feeling its way into the highly-competitive IT sector with first-class electronic data archiving and retrieval products which are sold under the TeleVault name and use the Group's expertise in high volume, secure data management.

Moving down the value chain, the division's network operation business is in full flow. Established as a means of protecting the Security Division's cash-in-transit vehicles, concerted external marketing has made the Datatrak vehicle location system a commercial success, with 14,000 UK subscribers. At home, customers include numerous regional ambulance services, while overseas Datatrak has found favour in Holland, Belgium and as far afield as Johannesburg and Buenos Aires.

In Datatrak and its other private mobile radio businesses, the division has both the best of the old and the most promising of new technologies. After developing its own private mobile radio system in the 1950s to communicate with its guards and patrol men, Securicor soon realised the potential of providing similar services to customers and developed the first network covering major trunk roads, a step which later led to integration with the AA radio network and eventually to Securicor's acquisition of the complete system in the mid-1960s.

The Datatrak vehicle location system in action

While Relayfone provided a system through which mobile phone users could communicate with a radio room which then passed on messages via land lines, Securicor also pioneered connection of a public access mobile radio network to the fixed-line telephone system through its Interconnect service, giving the division an understanding of market demand for mobile communications which would stand it in good stead when cellular arrived. Indeed, Relayfone endures to this day, alongside private mobile radio solutions designed for closed environments such as oil and chemicals plants.

At the cutting edge of mobile radio technology is linear modulation, a technique researched and developed by Securicor Communications which overcomes the problem of congestion on the air waves by reducing bandwidth from the worldwide standard of 12.5kHz to 5kHz. High-speed data transmission adds a host of possibilities for mobile radio users, including communication of video pictures, photographs and fingerprints.

Securicor's own needs have led it to the forefront of the technology, but development of linear modulation is also

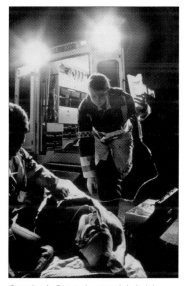

Securicor's Datatrak network is helping ambulances reach the scene of accidents more quickly

■

"We are in a high risk business, but there are many gems in the communications division. New opportunities continue to arise as customers require ever more sophisticated communications. Leading-edge technologies for both mobile and fixed-line services, coupled with partnerships and strategic alliances around the world, mean we can maximise our potential and seize those opportunities"

– Ed Hough

■

testament to the Group's commitment to challenging tomorrow's problems as well as providing today's solutions. The decision to invest in the technology, discovered at Bristol University under the auspices of the government's British Technology Group, was made back in 1988 and financial commitment has since been maintained.

Having spent years in research and development, however, the Communications Division's problem was not one of convincing prospective customers of the value of the technology, but reaching them in the first place. With 50 per cent of the forecast market for private mobile radio networks in the US, it was time to cross the Atlantic and put Securicor's name on the map in North America.

Aware of the often overwhelming problems faced by UK companies attempting to set up in North America, Roger Wiggs and Ed Hough crafted the vehicle which would pitch Securicor straight into the market. Federal Communications Commission approval was won for the technology and Securicor Radiocoms concluded its first technology licensing deal with US-based mobile radio supplier EF Johnson, beginning a partnership programme which would quickly spread the installation of linear modulation base stations across the country.

Activity is equally frenetic in the division's systems integration business, formed following the 1996 acquisition of Dopra, UK market leader in the supply of command and control systems for the emergency services and utilities. A natural implant into Securicor's overall profile as a key provider to these specific sectors, Dopra is already making a valuable profit contribution, taking advantage of its existing customer base and that of Securicor, as well as building on the skills of its 250 staff and adding new in-house and external product offerings to its toolbox.

While cellular and mobile communications, command and control systems and, to a degree, the division's electronics manufacturing capacity are natural adjuncts to the Group's traditional businesses, Hough is also building a portfolio of telecoms products and services which will stand or fall in the commercial market without recourse to a high level of internal business.

In concert with the Communications Division's other elements, however, the network supply link in the chain is being transformed from a traditional product supplier into a business response unit, able to provide customers with complete system solutions which will underpin their business strategies.

The 1983 acquisition of Robophone Communications gave the company an early entry into telephony, which was later strengthened by the purchase of part of Ferranti Business Systems in 1990 and the acquisition of Interconnect, a telephone systems designer and distributor in 1994.

Taking this one step further, Hough and his team were early to identify integrated services digital networks, which will accommodate everything from voice traffic to images and video conferencing, as an essential element of any full-service communications provider's promise. The division joined this potentially explosive market in 1993 through the acquisition of 3net. It has since gone on to expand both its European and Australian businesses, most recently purchasing the remaining 49 per cent of Securicor Network Dynamics, a New Zealand manufacturer of routers and bridgers for integrated services

Emergency service

Having tuned in to the Securicor Datatrak communications network in the spring of 1995, one regional ambulance service already claims significant reductions in the time taken to reach reported incidents.

Its 43 front-line ambulances are fitted with radio equipment linked to a central command and control system which is integrated with Datatrak. Emergency calls are logged directly into the system, which automatically triggers Datatrak to convert location information into a detailed Ordnance Survey reference for transmission to an operator's screen. Vehicle positions are updated every 13 seconds, allowing operators to make fast and effective decisions about which ambulances are best placed to attend particular accidents.

Using computerised versions of Ordnance Survey maps showing the positions of vehicles on streets on a scale of 1:10,000, Datatrak gives controllers a detailed picture of the locality, allowing them to guide vehicles to incidents in the minimum time, regardless of whether their crews are familiar with the area, thereby dramatically reducing the time patients must wait for an ambulance.

Providing an executive edge

With its fleet of 50 Mercedes Benz cars, used to convey busy corporate customers to and from appointments, one top-quality chauffeur-drive company based in the City of London has been working with Securicor Datatrak to develop a process which allows vehicles to respond to customers' immediate requests rather than handling jobs on a specified, pre-booked basis.

Using Datatrak has vastly improved the company's utilisation of its fleet, allowing controllers to monitor all car movements, match drivers to jobs as they arise and then guide them to their destinations with the aid of Datatrak's street-level mapping facility.

The company has developed in concert with Datatrak technology, progressing from cellular telephone and radio pager communication with its drivers to hand-held personal computers which will provide complete two-way data transmission.

Rewarding its faith in Datatrak, the business's sole problem with car theft was swiftly cleared up when a central controller relayed the stolen vehicle's movements to the police – the car was recovered in just six minutes.

digital networks, which supplies not only local markets but also customers in developing countries, including China.

Completing the portfolio, but only until Hough discovers another business opportunity, is Securicor Telesciences, a 1994 acquisition based in New Jersey, which collects line traffic information for communications network operators and which, in 1996, produced a profit of $3 million on turnover of $30 million. Ameritech, South Western Bell and US West have signed up for Telesciences services in the US and, if Hough's prognosis is correct, it won't be long before telecommunications carriers across the world want to follow their lead and improve customer knowledge to compete more successfully in deregulated markets.

Communications Division growth

	Turnover (£m) (excl. Cellnet)	Pre-tax profit (£m) (excl. Cellnet)
1992	63.6	(6.6)
1993	84.8	(4.5)
1994	148.9	(3.1)
1995	242.7	2.6*
1996	290.2	(4.5)*

*Profit before interest and taxation

COMMUNICATIONS DIVISION: THE PEOPLE

With over 10 years' experience in computer systems design, **Chris Forss** applies his expertise at Securicor Datatrak to develop new software applications for existing and potential users of the vehicle tracking and monitoring service both in the UK and overseas. As a senior software engineer he also works to support the network connecting Datatrak's five regional computer centres as well as links with customers.

"The best part of the job is tackling a new technical problem and solving it. The Datatrak vehicle positioning system already has a strong infrastructure, but now we're working to add value and attract new customers."

Based at the company's Swindon headquarters, Chris works as part of a team of engineers developing two-way radio communications for Datatrak, which is already used by a number of UK public service providers and has found success as far afield as Holland and Argentina.

Colin Wills joined ISDN communications specialist Securicor 3net in the late 1980s and weathered the company's transition from a venture capital start-up to becoming part of the Securicor Group. He now fills a sales support and product definition role, talking to customers to discover their requirements, before working with the company's own development team to ensure it is meeting market demand.

"This is a high-value, low-volume international business and the acquisition of 3net by Securicor has been a necessary part of the company's growth. The escalation in staff numbers from about 15 to nearer 100 changed the feel of working here, but the change created new opportunities and challenges for everyone in the company."

Using the experience he gained in 3net's hardware development group, Colin is a knowledgeable ambassador for the company and enjoys the additional customer contact and in-house communication which his current post entails.

Working for the past six years in the production area of Securicor Radiocoms' Midsomer Norton facility near Bath, **Margaret Brown** has progressed from printed circuit board assembly to a supervisory position. While she is still more than willing to lend a hand on the production line when deadlines are tight, most of her time is spent overseeing the 33 people working on printed circuit board assembly and scheduling the work which needs to be done.

Customers include in-house businesses such as Securicor Datatrak, but also major electronics consumers such as the Channel Tunnel and London Underground, which build Radiocoms products into their automatic signalling systems.

A global partnership

Liberalisation of the UK telecommunications network offered many expansion opportunities to international services and equipment suppliers but, with individual countries working to different telecoms standards, exploiting these possibilities is not easy. However, Securicor 3net has successfully helped one global communications systems business to make significant gains.

The integrated services digital network technology specialist within the Securicor Group, 3net developed a product which allows the US company's private branch exchange to interface to public networks as well as other private communication networks. Built around 3net's InterCHANGE technology, the card is manufactured in the UK for inclusion in private exchanges sold to large corporate users.

Since the first exchange products for the UK market went on sale in 1991, the relationship between the suppliers has been cemented with a technology partnership designed to provide the global communication systems business with an integrated and more cost-effective solution to the problems associated with ISDN connection.

■

"Communications is very different from the other divisions – we add value to technology while the others add value to people. The division is decentralised, with each managing director concentrating on his business. Staff numbers are relatively low at about 1,800, but with a higher ratio of graduates"

– Ed Hough

■

"The job is enjoyable and I get on well with people. On the whole, I find real job satisfaction in meeting orders," she says.

Dave Nicholls' job as a programme and project manager at Securicor Telecoms covers many activities, from working with major accounts installing telephony equipment and cabling to managing in-house change such as the introduction of a new computer system. He has been awarded a BABT approvals certificate, which allows him to approve new product features for use on the public telecommunications network and is busy surfing the Internet to discover its potential for the company.

"There's a new challenge every day and my bosses let me get on with the job. I've also done more travelling in recent years, which I enjoy."

Having joined Ferranti in 1970, Dave found himself working for Securicor after the latter bought some of Ferranti's business communications operations in 1990. In 1996 he received his 25-year service award at an event in Cambridge. "I felt like a youngster – everyone else on my table was there to receive a 30-year award!" he recalls.

Business services, more than any of Securicor's other divisions, reflects the expertise built up within the Group as it developed its security and distribution businesses. From vehicle maintenance to recruitment, these skills are no longer a matter only for internal scrutiny. Instead they are being put to the ultimate test of proving their worth in the commercial market.

Guiding development of the division until 1996, Chris Shirtcliffe was its chief architect, planning strategy for the disparate businesses, but always building with the common cause of the Group in mind. A Securicor veteran with a thorough knowledge of the Group, he joined the company's finance function in France in 1975 and worked both overseas and in the UK before settling in London in 1983 as group financial controller. With the retirement of Eric Hollis in 1985, he stepped on to the board as group financial director, the job on which he concentrates today having passed on responsibility for the Business Services Division in the 1996 group restructure.

As business services divisional chief executive, however, Shirtcliffe made his biggest contribution as an agent of change. In 1989, when he inherited the division then called Special Services, Shirtcliffe took on the Group's new joint venture in the recruitment business, Contract 2000; its long-established interest in The Richmond Hill and The Hylands hotels; the Group's computing operations; and the Phoenix travel agency.

Recruitment gave the division an instant boost, growing swiftly from two industrial recruitment bases in London to half a dozen branches by the end of 1989. But, with the recession beginning to bite at the turn of the decade, the good days were swiftly over and there was nothing to be done but batten down the hatches and sit out the storm.

It was not until 1992 that the recruitment business began to revive and, having held on to its interests through the recession, Securicor was well placed to meet demand. New branches were opened across the country and, as part of the Group's policy of turning successful internal businesses into commercial enterprises, a broader range of job types than those pertinent to Securicor's operations was covered.

Business Services

Chris Shirtcliffe, Group Financial Director

"For me, work is all about giving people happy, gainful employment, creating a worthwhile profit for shareholders and producing a product or service which is exactly what the customer needs. Being the biggest is not so important – if people enjoy their work, are challenged by it and do well, they will be well rewarded, as in turn our shareholders must be"

– Chris Shirtcliffe

While Securicor Recruitment Services still supplies specialist warehousemen, drivers and messengers, it has expanded into the general market for secretarial, administrative and clerical staff, as well as extending its geographic reach. In 1996, its national network of offices grew from 30 to over 50 sites, predominantly situated near out-of-town industrial and business centres rather than on the high street, with the aim of providing quality staff at reasonable prices.

The business proposition has been widely accepted, with Recruitment Services doubling its operating profit in 1996 and confident of making an even greater contribution to Business Services' pre-tax profit, which in 1996 reached £5.2 million. From the point of view of turning the customer focus around, the business has been a notable success, with over 90 per cent of annual turnover generated in the external market and total turnover representing almost half of the division's £77.3 million 1996 revenue.

The Group's hotels, for many years dedicated to company training, have also proved to have great potential. While Securicor had no intention of returning from whence it came and running a major hotel chain, The Richmond Hill Hotel in Surrey and The Hylands in Coventry were joined by The Richmond Gate Hotel in

1991. Adjacent to The Richmond Hill, Richmond Gate offered the possibilities of cost savings and efficiencies, which made the acquisition a classic example of the total being worth more than the sum of its parts.

Together with The Hylands, the Richmond hotels continued to provide some training facilities, although staff development opportunities were substantially enhanced by the acquisition of the Hartsfield Manor management training centre in Surrey which, again, is used both as an internal resource and marketed to external clients.

At the hotels, a leisure complex opened at The Richmond Hill Hotel in the summer of 1996 immediately paid dividends as the company raised room rates and attracted new customers. Far from a Securicor stronghold, the Richmond hotels are now primarily used by non-related companies and individuals and can claim higher than average room occupancy, a further fillip to turnover and profit. In Coventry, the 50-bedroom Hylands is also looking to improve profit margins through plans to develop its 100-seat restaurant to appeal more directly to non-residents as well as those staying at the hotel.

The paring down of Securicor's five divisions to four in the early 1990s and the merger of Transport with Special Services to form the Business Services Division, created the most difficult challenge faced by Chris Shirtcliffe and his team. A centre of excellence and a critical component of Securicor's Security and Distribution Divisions, the transport division had little experience in the commercial market and even less as a stand-alone profit and loss business.

Included in the division were many remnants from the past, some sound acquisitions in their time but of less value for the future, others with a history of being exclusively internal suppliers. The car and truck dealerships RJ Bown and Chiswick Garage, bought to ensure a steady supply of Ford vehicles for Securicor's own fleet, were no longer a necessity when vehicle manufacture moved into overcapacity and were subsequently sold.

Vehicle Services and the company's 600 vehicle maintenance staff, however, were considered strategically important within the

A picture of success

A world-class film specialist chooses The Richmond Hill Hotel to accommodate its guests – both individual visitors and international conference delegates. Only a few miles from the company's headquarters, the hotel has always been considered a far more comfortable and friendly option than the huge impersonal airport hotels.

The company has been working with The Richmond Hill Hotel and The Richmond Gate Hotel for over 20 years, building a strong yet flexible relationship. Both bedrooms and conference facilities are regularly booked for both local and overseas staff and guests, the hotel hosting executives from the company's worldwide subsidiaries when it selected the UK as the location for its international conference in 1994.

The hotel's friendly staff, comfortable environment and obliging service are not the only attraction, according to visitors. Situated in the royal borough of Richmond, the hotel provides easy access to the town centre as well as the recreational activities offered by Richmond Park and the nearby Thames, plus a variety of night-life to suit all tastes.

The road to service

With thousands of tow trucks and small vans constantly on the road, one of the major providers of roadside help to vehicle owners has been working with Securicor Vehicle Services for several years in a reciprocal partnership designed to improve the efficiency and cost-effectiveness of servicing its own fleet.

Building on a long-standing relationship between the customer and Securicor's parcel delivery and cash-in-transit operations, the contract resulted from top-level discussions when both companies were reviewing their service centre networks. Under the agreement, Securicor services vehicles in areas not covered by the customer's depots in return for an equivalent service for Securicor vehicles beyond the reach of in-house service centres.

Both Securicor and its partner report that the rationalisation scheme has brought advantages, with the companies' high visibility and equal commitment to quality of service leading to similar expectations of work carried out.

With rationalisation a constant business process, there is no doubt that the benefits of sharing resources will gradually augment the current agreement.

Group and ripe for commercial exploitation. What they lacked was market-oriented management, a problem solved by the appointment from outside Securicor of Alan Hines as managing director. Creating a leaner organisation was his first priority, making some lay-offs and workshop closures inevitable.

By 1996, Securicor Vehicle Services was managing and maintaining the Group's own fleet of towards 10,000 vehicles, as well as 3,000 vehicles belonging to external customers. Diversification into commercial hire, a deal with Iveco on truck rental and an internal contract hire business for company cars helped to push up turnover, as did the 1995 addition of Rentmaster and Fuelserv, profitable businesses acquired as part of the Russell Davies purchase.

Bedwas Bodyworks, for so long a supplier of vehicles to the Security and Distribution Divisions, became a non-core operation and was sold at a modest profit in June 1996.

Change and growth within the division, coupled to the Group restructure, also led to the change in management which saw

Chris Shirtcliffe relinquish his role as business services' divisional chief executive in 1996.

Far from leaving the division without a rudder, however, group chief executive Roger Wiggs replaced Shirtcliffe with seasoned managers and reorganised its businesses to reflect their market strengths. Computer Services, once solely an in-house concern but more recently a third-party supplier, moved to the Communications Division, while Alan Hines took over Securicor Vehicle Services and its subsidiaries and Jeff Pack, in addition to his role as group treasurer, was awarded executive charge of the hotels and recruitment business.

If meeting the ebb and flow of market demand was the initial raison d'être of the Business Services Division, it had to watch a few of its operations go out on the tide. RJ Bown and Chiswick Garage were a case in point. Another adaptation to changing circumstances is evidenced by the history of Phoenix World Travel. Acquired in the early 1980s to organise and profit from the rising amount of travel undertaken by Securicor executives, in its heyday it operated a successful high-street outlet at the company's Victoria offices. The Group's move to Sutton in 1988, however, ended its public presence and Phoenix made the return journey from commercial competitor to in-house specialist supplier.

Setting aside this minor digression from the division's strategy, the transition from internal supplier to external market force was

Alan Hines, Managing Director, Securicor Vehicle Services

■

"Our transport businesses have turned very much from being internal suppliers to external market providers. Fuelserv, Rentmaster and the Eurotruck contract hire operation we run with Iveco are expanding very rapidly. By developing new products we will have a growing involvement in the market over coming years"

– Alan Hines

■

Business Services Division growth

	Turnover (£m)	Pre-tax profit (£m)
1992	13.4	5.6
1993	24.4	6.8
1994	31.2	6.2
1995	48.7	5.0*
1996	77.3	14.5*

*Profit before interest and taxation

Jeff Pack, Group Treasurer

complete, begging the question of how to maintain and improve internal group functions. The solution was in the formation of Securicor Management Services. Chaired by company secretary Nigel Griffiths, the business acts as an umbrella for all divisions, including group functions such as accounting and finance, legal, personnel policy, training and information technology. Its remit is to ensure Securicor gains full value from group costs. The story of its predecessor suggests it may also prove fertile ground for nurturing new business initiatives, although its early emphasis will be on excellence of service and cost efficiency.

BUSINESS SERVICES DIVISION: THE PEOPLE

Hazel Simpson is a familiar face to regular guests of The Richmond Hill Hotel, but also works hard behind the scenes to make sure that every visitor's stay is enjoyable. Having taken her first job with the group as a receptionist at the hotel in 1980, Hazel has progressed to become reception manager. Her tasks include everything from room allocation to invoice checking, taking in staff management and the writing of daily reports along the way.

"Over my years at the hotel it has changed completely. Every day is different and there is always something exciting around the corner, for example the opening of the Cedars health club at The Richmond Gate Hotel."

Hazel enjoys the challenge of meeting customer requirements, but is also keen to give staff some of the opportunities she has had within Securicor. A training and development programme for the hotel's 10 receptionists is under way, with a view to securing an Investor in People award.

Securicor Recruitment Services has blossomed in recent years and now operates over 50 offices nationwide. At Salford Quays in Manchester, office services consultant **Stephanie Byrne** starts early to make sure all the day's temporary jobs are filled. Then it is on with the business of interviewing potential employees, working out wages and visiting customers.

"We have an average of over 80 temporary staff out working on any one day and I also take some part in hiring permanent recruits. I used to work in a smaller agency, but have enjoyed being able to progress with a larger company and now have an assistant working for me."

Meantime, in Cheltenham, driving and industrial specialist **Georgina Herbert** is filling temporary vacancies for anything from mailroom packers to HGV drivers, placing about 50 staff a day as well as working with customers wanting to take on permanent employees.

"Having worked as a sales rep for 10 years, moving to recruitment gave me a chance to work on the service side. I really like the constant contact with other people and there is nothing more satisfying than filling a booking with someone who will meet the customer's requirement."

"The Cedars health and leisure club developed adjacent to The Richmond Hill and The Richmond Gate hotels is a huge success, not only supporting occupancy and room rates in the hotels but also attracting an external membership of about 1,300 local residents. One of the best clubs in the country, Cedars certainly matches our initial idea of enhancing the hotels' facilities and creating a profit centre in its own right"

– Jeff Pack

■

"Through the development of our staff we can offer a total package of top-quality integrated services to customers worldwide, at the same time giving a good return to all stakeholders in the company"

– Henry McKay

■

■

"Working for Securicor becomes more than a job – it's a way of life. Drivers wear a uniform and feel part of the company, long-service and loyalty are recognised at frequent awards ceremonies and over 50 staff have made it to the One Million Milers Club, a journey which takes about 15 years"

– Pat Howes

■

■

"For me, work is all about giving people happy, gainful employment, creating a worthwhile profit for shareholders and producing a product or service which is exactly what the customer needs. Being the biggest is not so important – if people enjoy their work, are challenged by it and do well, they will be well rewarded, as in turn our shareholders must be"

– Chris Shirtcliffe

■

THE GLOBAL PERSPECTIVE

5

THE GLOBAL PERSPECTIVE

With a roster of 40 overseas operations, Securicor can rightly claim multinational status and offer customers the best of both worlds – top-quality services in domestic and international markets.

The route to this point has not always been smooth, however, and Keith Erskine's initial global ambitions suffered as many failures as successes. But they did fire the company's management with the enthusiasm and drive to keep breaking new ground, despite the many problems of setting up in unfamiliar territory. As a result the Group's expertise and reputation have become recognised worldwide. Security operations are to the fore within the Pacific Rim, Europe, Africa and the Americas, while distribution services are provided in Europe, Africa and the Pacific Rim. US interests also grew as the Communications Division found a foothold and rapidly expanded into the mobile radio network market.

The task of directing Securicor's international security business falls to Securicor Security Services' divisional chief executive, Henry McKay. His inheritance included operations in 16 countries. In Africa a solid guarding, cash-in-transit and parcels business had been developed, while in the Far East Securicor had built a reputation predominantly around its cash-in-

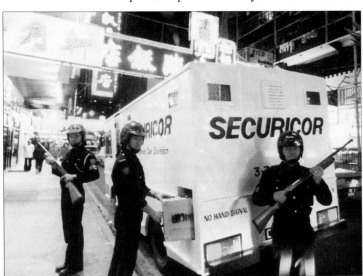

transit and guarding services. Elsewhere, a somewhat piecemeal approach had created business units initially with a will and a way of their own, but soon to be brought into the fold.

A close survey of existing and potential markets following divisionalisation led to the redrawing of Securicor's world map and was also instrumental in putting up signposts to new destinations. Indeed, the international business is nothing if not confident, targeting to bring in 50 per cent of the Security Division's total profits by the year 2000.

By 1995, when Securicor celebrated its 25th anniversary of working in Africa, the company could claim a turnover contribution of £14 million from the region, a figure which continues to grow. The African adventure started, however, following encouragement from Keith Erskine's brother Derek, who lived in Kenya, to take on a contract for the supply of Alsatian guard dogs to Angola's Benguela Railway Company. The dogs were duly trained in England and transported to Benguela to protect cargo on the 800-mile train journey across the continent. Their role was both to track thieves and sniff out frightened crew who deserted the train and took to the bush when bandits struck. Notwithstanding the constant threat of malcontent marauders on two legs and four, the contract was a success and, following extensive groundwork by John Allen, Roger Wiggs was sent to set up a permanent operation in Kenya. Securicor (Uganda) followed, although it was later lost when Idi Amin took over the country in 1971 and sequestered many overseas businesses. Next Wiggs travelled to Malawi, setting up Securicor (Malawi), and then on to Zambia, where he bought a security firm in the copper belt and formed Securicor (Copperbelt), while Securicor (Zambia) was installed in Lusaka.

Other countries were considered but abandoned for lack of potential business, strong competition or political instability, while some small start-ups ground to a halt when local business proved too slow or dangerous.

However, the apparently promising future of the four established enterprises in Africa prompted Erskine to create a new subsidiary, Securicor Global, which acted as an umbrella for all overseas business and eventually evolved into Securicor International, with its four regions of Africa, the Far East, the Americas, and Europe and the Middle East. Each offers core cash-handling and guarding services, while some have added unique local services.

By 1997, the African contingent of Kenya, Zambia and Malawi employed over 17,000 guards and operated around 500 vehicles out of its branch network. The majority of the business remains in static guarding, but Kenya also runs a sizeable parcel delivery operation, and all three supply a radio response service for alarmed premises.

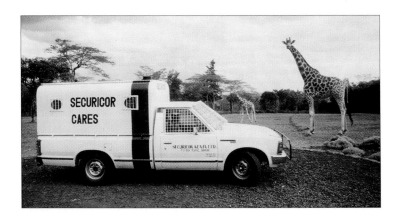

Expansion and consolidation is also a constant priority in Europe, although fierce competition, government-owned monopolies and a plethora of local laws and restrictions made Europe a very difficult region to conquer in all business respects.

As in Africa, the Europe and Middle East region also faced specific challenges and some insurmountable problems. An operation in Kuwait survived the Iraqi invasion of 1990, but not without some trauma (*see the entries from George Woodberry's diary at the end of the chapter*); the company had to abandon its work in Cyprus when the island was divided; and it took two attempts to secure a foothold in Malta after the first was denied a licence to continue trading by the Dom Mintoff regime.

The 1990s acquisition and joint venture programme masterminded by Henry McKay, however, did much to spread the net and gave Securicor a strong presence across Western Europe as well as bases in Turkey, Russia and Hungary. Closer to home, and with much experience already behind them, the offshore islands, such as Jersey, Guernsey and the Isle of Man, continued to do brisk and lucrative business.

Contributing over £140 million worth of business by 1996, Europe and the Middle East provided proof of the wisdom of expansion through acquisition, enlarging the Securicor network as well as encouraging countries providing selected services to advance into new markets. Germany, by way of example, extended its lead in guarding through the major acquisition of

ASD, but maintains a policy which takes it into services such as alarm monitoring through further acquisitions or partnerships. Elsewhere in Europe, Securicor maintains a careful watch for opportunities to provide first response alarm services as individual countries pass the responsibility from law enforcement agencies to the private sector.

Like any international development, constraints on growth are not in identifying new potential but in securing the necessary investment and people resources. Development director of Security Services, Ann Perkins, receives an enquiry every week from somewhere in the world about joining forces with Securicor. While many of the offers are attractive, only a few are pursued.

With such limitations in mind, Securicor has built its security business in the Americas through well-orchestrated joint ventures and acquisitions. An initial 12 branches, 100 vehicles and 1,000 employees laid foundations for the future, Securicor's arrival in the Americas marking the more formal development of ideas sparked by Erskine during his chairmanship.

A venture into Jamaica in 1971 showed promise as Securicor scooped 90 per cent of local cash-carrying business from US competitors and prepared to purchase an established guarding and patrolling business. In a not unusual *volte face*, however, Erskine pulled the plug at the last moment, this time for the sound reasons of deteriorating law and order on the island and increasing pressure on sterling, which made a far-flung entity such as the Jamaican business difficult to integrate in the overseas portfolio. Securicor's operations in Mauritius, Swaziland and Ethiopia were also closed as a result of the currency squeeze.

The cyclical nature of business brought happier news from Jamaica by the mid-1990s, however, when Securicor reopened to service the local market. Bases in Costa Rica and Barbados have also been developed, while existing operations in Venezuela, Trinidad and Guyana continue to thrive, albeit in a completely different fashion to their counterparts elsewhere in the world. Pump-action shotguns and side arms feature in South America, as they do in Hong Kong and the Pacific region, whereas staff in Africa carry no arms and, in Europe, fire power is prohibited by local legislation, with the exception of France where legislation requires each cash-in-transit vehicle to carry at least three firearms.

While firearms are an essential part of the job in the Americas, local knowledge has proved equally invaluable. Entering Trinidad's security market in the mid-1980s, Securicor joined forces with Caribbean trading conglomerate Neal & Massy, providing services not only to its 90 member companies, but also to their customers. A branch in Barbados was quick to follow, before a partnership with Thomas Greg & Son in Columbia extended the business to Costa Rica and the Dominican Republic.

A member of the rare but growing breed of women who have reached the highest echelons of business management, Ann Perkins became the commercial director of Securicor Limited in 1988 and has since completed 30 years with the group.

In the male-dominated environment of security services she made her presence felt, initiating wage-packeting before setting up the thriving banking support services operation in 1982 and later leading Securicor's international business into uncharted territories. Her fund of energy and ideas is far from exhausted.

"We are taking the next giant leap forward, from working in cash handling to specialising in cash management. For example, we are developing real-time cash

counting and reporting, as well as supplier partnerships which would allow us to offer full service solutions such as complete automated teller machine operation.

"Such services can often be exported, particularly to countries like the Americas which, having been behind in development terms, are now crying out for banking services.

"There are geographic areas as diverse as Columbia, Costa Rica, Russia and Turkey where we have recently arrived and are beginning to attract local business. That's not to deny that we are constantly reviewing other possibilities as well.

"North America, for example, already has more than its share of guarding companies, but I see niche market opportunities. There is a lot of interest in UK-style privatisation of prisons and prison services. Obviously our domestic custodial experience would be a benefit and, with the right local partner, Securicor would be well placed to enter the market."

Banking services, including cash-in-transit, are much in demand, as well as airport, factory and office guarding. With turnover running at around £24.4 million a decade later, Securicor believes the Americas are ripe for expansion in both geographic and business terms.

On the other side of the world, the Asia-Pacific region has more than borne out early forecasts of a strong and developing market for security services. A joint venture under the Jardine Securicor name can claim turnover in excess of £100 million – a far cry from Erskine's tentative approach in 1962 when he sent his first envoy to Malaysia.

Indeed, the excursion to Malaysia made a slow start, but gathered pace through the remainder of the 1960s as the business made ground with local banks which sought protection from isolated groups of terrorists who threatened their vehicles carrying money to outlying rubber plantations and tin mining areas. Securicor sent its first two cash-in-transit vans modified for the tropics to the peninsula in 1962 and, thereafter, the fleet continued to expand, in later years with the addition of Hong Kong made vehicles.

This early foothold in Malaysia was enough, however, to set Erskine's ambitions alight once more. In 1964, an attempt to open in Thailand was thwarted by a potential partner's insistence on owning 51 per cent of the shares in the proposed company and a machine gun attack on the branch, although an office was successfully opened in Singapore. Not long after, a base was established in Hong Kong, but it was two months before Securicor won its first contract with Taylor Woodrow, which was embarking on construction of the Hong Kong Ocean Terminal.

Things looked up dramatically when Securicor fortuitously found itself in the right place at the right time. A terrorist bomb attack on the Hong Kong & Shanghai Banking Corporation opposite Securicor's office provided the opportunity to supply an emergency four-man guard. Within a week, the bank's head office had negotiated a contract for security protection of all its 18 branches, lifting Securicor Hong Kong out of the red and placing it firmly in the local business directory.

By 1977, the property protection operation had extended to cash carrying and a newly formed alarms division won the prestigious contract to design, install and maintain an alarm system for the world's largest privately financed housing project, the 100, 20-storey tower blocks accommodating 90,000 people at Mei Foo Sun Chuen.

With Hong Kong and Malaysia over their teething troubles, Securicor returned to Thailand in 1983 to set up a successful joint venture, securing a contract to guard the Thai Shell Exploration site 250 miles north of Bangkok.

Elsewhere in the region, an outlet in Macau delivered its initial promise and, like its counterpart in Hong Kong, supplies not only local services but also cash-carrying operations for the business and industrial areas of the People's Republic of China, a market which has interesting growth potential following reunification with Hong Kong.

Indeed, since its formation in 1990, Jardine Securicor has been building on its reputation as the largest security services business in south east Asia. To the old-established operations were added a base in Indonesia, making Securicor the country's only commercial armoured vehicle operator, and a purpose-built branch in Taipei, offering guarding and cash-transport services throughout Taiwan.

It is not just geographical expansion from which Securicor plans to benefit in the Far East. Like other regional divisions, it

constantly monitors local markets with a view to augmenting services with those available elsewhere in the world – not to mention developing additional options to meet international customers' constantly evolving needs.

Africa revisited

Sir Ranulph Bacon, chairman of Securicor Global in the 1970s, included in his duties many overseas visits, among them a tour of inspection to east Africa in early 1970. On his return to the UK he summed up his impressions in an editorial for *Securicor Guardian*:

"If it is thought that Securicor is growing fast in Great Britain – as of course it is – we have got quite a job to keep up with our rate of expansion in Africa.

"Only two or three years ago, Kenya was one stronghold. Now we are established in four other countries with every prospect of adding more. There are seven branches in Kenya, nine in Uganda, 11 in Zambia, two in Malawi and one in Ethiopia.

"Part of this boom arises from the discovery by the inhabitants that they can now get house guards who are trained in their job, manage to keep awake, are regularly supervised and are not in league with thieves. My previous experience of this type of watchman in tropical countries was that they had none of these advantages. If a home was broken into, the almost automatic assumption was that the guard was asleep, or had been primed with liquor, or was doing some courting somewhere else, even if he was not the number one suspect as the tipper-off of the thieves.

"In Nairobi, some 1,400 guards go on duty every night. I hasten to add that some proportion of these are, of course, engaged at commercial premises and industrial plants. And, lest this may sound like a 'soft number' in a pleasant place, these men do a 12-hour stint with, in many cases, a walk of some miles to and from it.

"The other main duty of our African branches is the transport of cash. Not quite as we know it, as so much is over long distances with sometimes rough and very lonely roads. A raiding gang may muster 30 legs between them, together with bundooks. In Uganda, where the kind of country lends itself to easy ambush, our guards have firearms too, but even that may not be enough.

"One of our busiest areas is the copper belt in Zambia, and here I found wholly unexpected conditions. Copper slag, because of its fluorescence, looks gorgeous in the moonlight but ghastly in daylight. By no stretch of the imagination can our own mining

towns be called attractive, yet planners in Zambia have contrived the landscape to look like rural pastures."

Life in the fast lane

Andy Nicol, chief operations officer of the Jardine Securicor joint venture formed in 1990 and the leading security services business in south east Asia, is an enthusiastic promoter of both Securicor's long-term operations in the Far East and its ventures in emerging markets such as Indonesia and Taiwan.

He may be a long way from home, but Nicol has certainly seen the world in his 28 years with the company. Having been brought up in Scotland, he applied to join Securicor in 1967. But, aged only 20, he was five years off the company's minimum age limit and had to dismiss the idea. When a patrol van turned up at his home, delivered him to the local branch where he was issued with a uniform, set of keys and a guard dog and told to set out on patrol, his luck had turned. From a part-time post, he soon graduated to become a full-time patrol officer and management trainee.

His first overseas posting took him to Kenya from 1979 to 1981, before he was seconded for a year to set up business in Trinidad and Tobago. In fact, he ran the Caribbean venture formed with Neal & Massy for five years – opening a location in Venezuela along the way – prior to transferring to Hong Kong in 1990.

"I feel as if I'm in the right place at the right time – this is a very dynamic area of the world. Besides regular services such as guarding, cash-in-transit and cash management, we also offer some one-offs. In Hong Kong, for example, we run south east Asia's largest coin-processing centre, handling 20 tons of coins a day for the colony's unique transport network, which includes ferries between the island and mainland, as well as connecting tunnels and the Mass Transit Railway.

"We also supply special guards for race meetings at the Royal Hong Kong Jockey Club, controlling course security as well as collecting cash from numerous off-site betting shops.

"We're exceptionally proud of the unique guarding service we offer using ex-Gurkha military men. When the regiment was disbanded, we recruited a number of its officers in Nepal and brought them to Hong Kong as premier league guards. They're fantastic people and very popular among our blue chip commercial customers.

"Besides the Gurkhas in Hong Kong, all employees in the rest of the region are local, as most countries in the Far East don't allow labour to be imported. That has its problems in places such as Malaysia, where there is virtually zero unemployment, but works well in countries such as Thailand, which have a tradition of military service.

"Indeed, understanding and adhering to local customs is as important when doing business in the Far East as being able to offer required services."

Keeping up in Kenya

Les Winter is deputy managing director of Securicor Kenya having climbed up through the ranks from the role of officer patrolman. This three-year contract is not his first stint overseas – he has previously experienced working life in both Kuwait and Hungary – but he numbers his days in Africa among the most satisfying during his career with the company.

From Securicor's regional headquarters in Nairobi, Winter describes a business environment much advanced from that outlined earlier by Sir Ranulph Bacon but a similar ethos, which leads most who have worked there to look back with nostalgia.

"There are over 10,000 Securicor employees in Kenya these days, the majority working on guarding assignments. Unlike the UK, guard dogs are a fundamental part of the operation, working on both business and residential guarding contracts.

"Besides guarding, we also operate alarm response, cash-in-transit and courier services, with local branch managers reporting to me here in Nairobi. Some branches are in very remote and isolated locations and they have to adapt to the environment, but in the city

business is run along much the same lines as elsewhere. Customers range from individual property owners to multinationals such as Total Oil, Esso, Standard Chartered and Barclays Bank.

"Kenya is a beautiful country and the people are lovely, but it's about ten years behind the UK, which means there's a lot of stress in just achieving what colleagues at home would consider basic business skills. That said, I'm very proud to be working for Securicor Africa and find the job more challenging than anything else I have tackled so far."

The Great Escape

When George Woodberry, operations director of Securicor International, travelled to Kuwait in the summer of 1990 to cover the general manager's home leave, he could not have foreseen the perils he was to face. On 2nd August, 1990, Iraqi troops invaded the country. Throughout the 10 days he remained in Kuwait and during the 24-hour dash across the desert to Saudi Arabia, Woodberry kept a detailed diary.

2nd August, 1990 – Kuwait invaded by Iraqi troops and tanks just before dawn

07.15　　Arrived at branch. Instructed all cash-in-transit vehicles back to base.

09.10   Removed "Security" from sign outside, plus Kuwaiti flag.

10.10   Last but one of vehicles with cash on board back in base. Still five vehicles (four empty) out.

11.00   Four empty vehicles still not returned. One vehicle which did return had been raided by Iraqis and the radio ripped out. Crews of other four possibly held for questioning – may think we are some type of government security (or police).

12.30   Received call from Roger Wiggs (London). Advised him of situation.

13.30   Last vehicle with cash on board back, but still empty vans missing.

13.45   Instructed all cash-in-transit and admin staff to leave branch.

14.30   One more vehicle back. Three still stranded, crew of one accounted for.

14.45   Another crew accounted for – one three-man crew still missing.

15.00   Decided to secure and evacuate branch rather than risk lives.

15.15   Curfew announced. Advised all guards still on duty to remain at assignments.

3rd August, 1990

08.00   Still no news of three missing cash-in-transit crew men.

4th August, 1990

16.00   Went to branch, all secure. Recovered two vehicles, one with a number of bullet holes. Three crew men still missing.

5th August, 1990

Troops have dug in around area of branch including installation of field guns. Branch will remain secure but unmanned. Food is starting to be a problem.

6th August, 1990

Staff passports removed from branch to give out to staff who want them.

New government has stated that normal working will commence today. Due to threat to Brits and other Europeans they should remain indoors. Kept branch closed down, unmanned.

7th August, 1990

16.00   Guards have taken two staff hostage, demanding their wages. Gave full authorisation for them to be paid, but will not risk lives for sake of money.

Tried to get to branch, but turned back by troops. The staff may demand all cash in the vaults (approx. KD1.3 million). If that happens I will have no alternative but to give the go ahead, especially as 40 staff are cash-in-transit operatives who know what is in the vaults.

22.00   Advised that the head office of our partner, Al Mulla, has been gutted following an attempt to blow the safe.

8th August, 1990

Attempted to get to branch, but again stopped by troops. Concerned about staff held hostage for pay.

Now one of seven adults and two children sharing a basement apartment with enough food for about a month.

Iraqis looting shops, gold souks, banks and companies. Food will be increasingly difficult to obtain. Our supervisors are also bringing food – total company loyalty.

9th August, 1990

All staff have been paid full dues. Management staff have been freed. Evacuated branch until further notice.

10th August, 1990

Consider making a run for the Saudi border, but no confirmation of any successful crossings. We will not take the risk unless things get really bad here.

11th August, 1990

Have had confirmation that 45 to 50 Europeans have crossed the border into Saudi and on to Bahrain. Only another 3,950 of us Brits to get out!

Again looking for a Bedouin guide to make an attempt ourselves, but the BBC World Service announcement of the escapees will probably mean the Iraqis will tighten the net across the border.

22.00 Understand from a contact that the last British and Kuwaiti employees have made a run for it. This will make my decision easier as, especially if they make it – I feel I have no further responsibilities here other than the company assets and cash, which there is not a lot I can do about.

12th August, 1990

We are unable to contact a Bedouin to guide us across the desert, but have decided to go for it anyway, despite the shooting of a Brit at the border yesterday. Embassy advice to abandon any attempts and Iraqi patrols along the route; our adrenalin is pumping. We are a convoy of seven vehicles and 21 people.

13.10 We are on our way. Down the sixth and on to the seventh ring, passing the back of the airport and on to the desert. Distance travelled, 70km.

14.15   10km into the desert we are confronted by an Iraqi patrol. A Kuwaiti in the lead car bribes the soldiers with fruit and a case of soft drinks.

14.30   Happen upon a Bedouin camp. Told we are in the right direction for the border, but there is soft sand ahead.

14.50   Find the soft sand and skirt around it, but not certain where we are until we come across a dirt track going north to south. A number of civilian vehicles pointing south are stationary. We assume this is a security checkpoint and head back across the desert to avoid it. Two further cars have joined us. We are now nine vehicles and 25 people. Temperature 120°F.

15.15   We have hit soft sand, three vehicles are bogged down. After 45 minutes of digging, pushing and pulling, we get all out. We decide to try another direction. Again we drive in the general direction of south/south west, keeping the sun on our right hand side. An hour later we drive over a rise in a fan formation to be confronted by eight Iraqi tanks. Without speaking we change our formation to a line and drive at a steady speed through the two middle tanks. As the troops seem to make no sudden movement, we continue driving through. Terrified!

17.45   We see ahead what seems to be a hill the breadth of the desert. On getting closer it is found to be a 20 foot sand wall with a ditch on the other side – probably anti-tank. We can see nothing but desert in all directions. We decide to take a chance and turn right following the wall. After about 2km we see a gap in the wall and men in uniform – Saudis or Iraqis? We drive on towards the soldiers. They are Saudis – we have made it!

Suddenly We were the only Brits to make a successful escape that day.

THE FINANCIAL PERFORMANCE

6

THE FINANCIAL PERFORMANCE

The charts on the following pages provide a visual demonstration of Securicor's growth, from a faltering start to the streamlined and strategically planned expansion of latter years.

While documented evidence of the company's results in its formative years as Night Watch Services and later Night Guards is sketchy owing to its private status, statistics following the 1960 acquisition of Securicor by the Erskine family's successful hotel business begin to provide a clearer view of its fortunes. However, it should be noted that prior to 1970 little financial information was required to be published by law. Hence, figures shown for the period should be read as estimates.

From a loss in 1961, Securicor's first year trading as a subsidiary of Kensington Palace Hotel Limited, the sibling of Denys Erskine's Associated Hotels Limited, the company turned in a profit by year three and has never since looked back. Indeed, by 1967 the security business eclipsed that of its parent, providing 73 per cent of pre-tax profit and 60 per cent of the pre-tax profit reported by the group company, Associated Hotels.

When the Kensington Palace group broke the £1 million profit barrier in 1970, 80 per cent of which was contributed by Securicor, it was time to part company with the hotel businesses. In 1973 a buyer was found, the tow ropes were dropped and Securicor set sail.

Total Shareholder Return

TOP TSR PERFORMERS 1966–1995

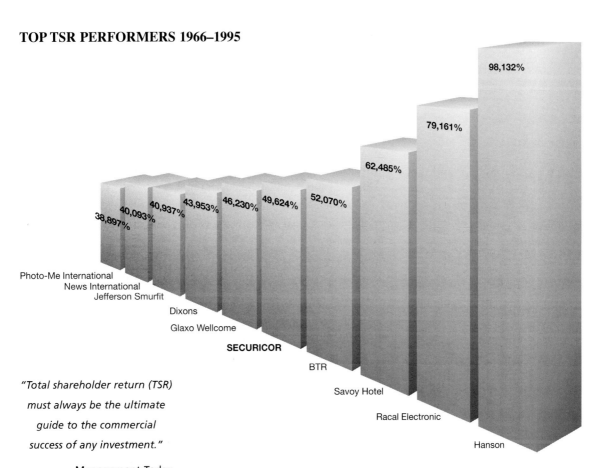

"Total shareholder return (TSR) must always be the ultimate guide to the commercial success of any investment."

– Management Today

"As a director of a public company I must maximise the value of shares as well as look after our employees and consider the public good."

– Roger Wiggs

A Financial History:
The Big Picture

TURNOVER

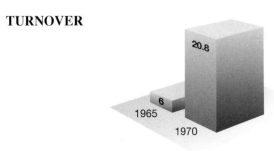

*Securicor's contribution to
Associated Hotels' total
turnover (£m)*

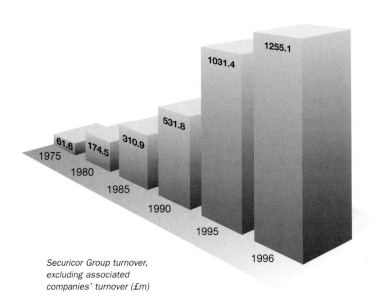

*Securicor Group turnover,
excluding associated
companies' turnover (£m)*

PROFIT BEFORE TAXATION

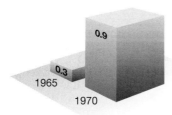

*Securicor's contribution to
Associated Hotels' profit before
taxation (£m)*

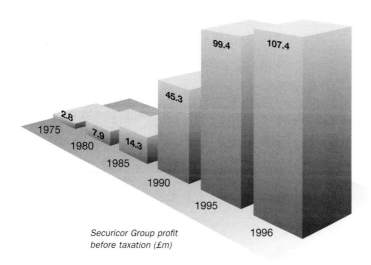

*Securicor Group profit
before taxation (£m)*

Focus on Ten Years:
Exponential Growth

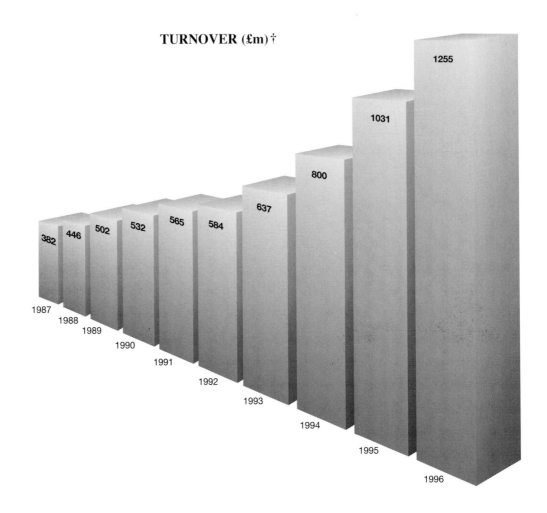

TURNOVER (£m) †

† *Excluding associated companies' turnover.*

PRE-TAX PROFIT (£m)

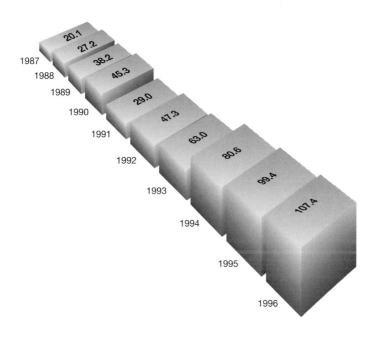

Year	Value
1987	20.1
1988	27.2
1989	38.2
1990	45.3
1991	29.0
1992	47.3
1993	63.0
1994	80.6
1995	99.4
1996	107.4

CAPITAL EMPLOYED (£m)

Year	Value
1987	108.6
1988	102.8
1989	136.6
1990	191.3
1991	211.6
1992	240.0
1993	270.9
1994	311.1
1995	404.3
1996	502.0

Focus on Five Years: Group Development

AVERAGE MARKET CAPITALISATION (£m)

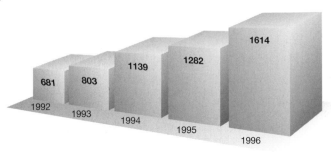

EARNINGS PER SHARE (pence)

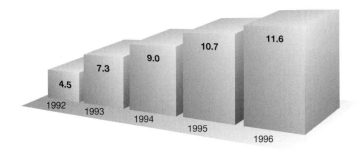

NET ASSETS (£m)/RETURN (%)

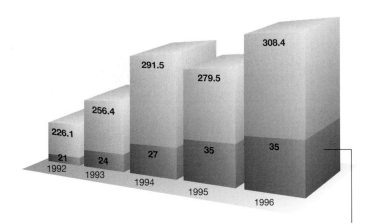

Percentage return on assets

VEHICLE FLEET

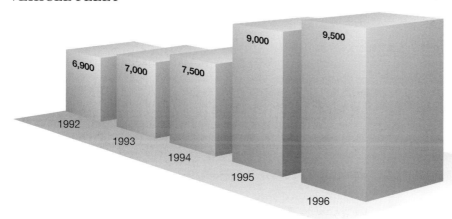

EMPLOYEES

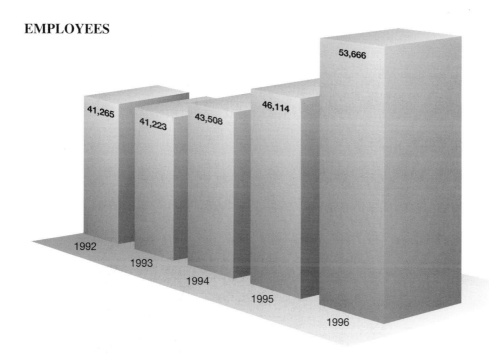

Developing Divisions: 1992–1996

TURNOVER (£m)

Security*

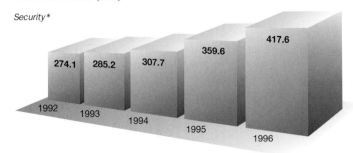

Distribution

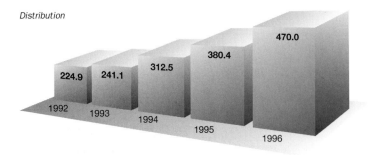

Communications (excluding Cellnet)

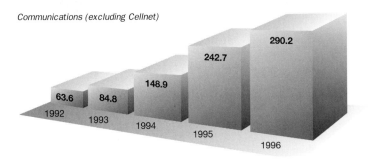

Business Services

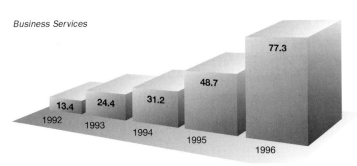

PROFIT BEFORE TAXATION (£m)†

Security

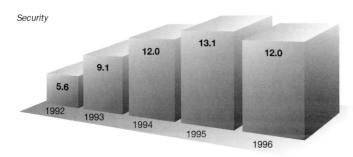

Distribution

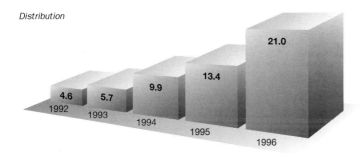

Communications

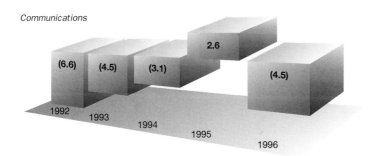

Business Services

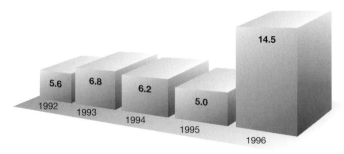

Cellnet

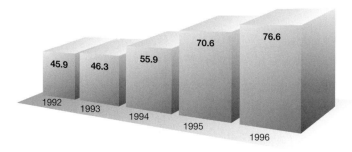

* Excluding associated companies' turnover.

† 1995 and 1996 figures show profit before interest and taxation.

Global Growth

TURNOVER (£m)

United Kingdom

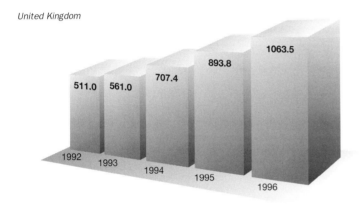

Rest of Europe*

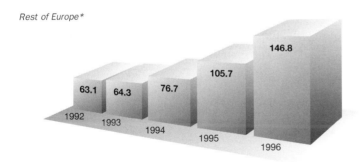

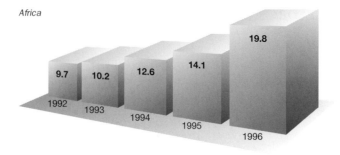

Africa

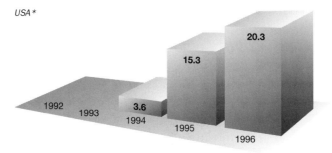

USA*

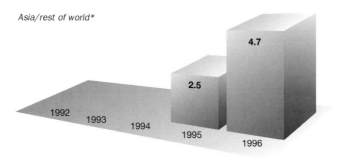

Asia/rest of world*

* Excluding associated companies' turnover.

PROFIT BEFORE TAXATION (£m)†

United Kingdom

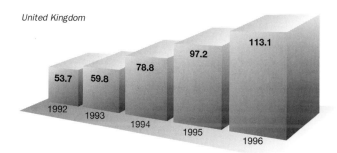

Rest of Europe

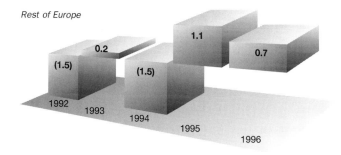

Africa

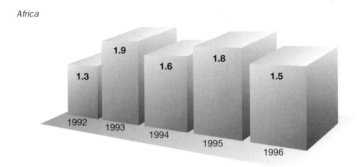

USA

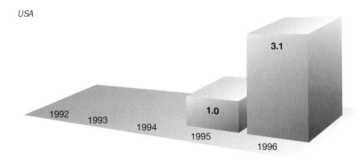

Asia/rest of the world

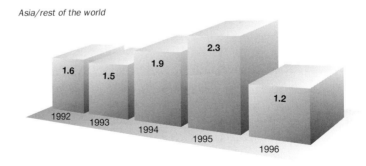

† 1995 and 1996 figures show profit before interest and taxation.

Principal developments since June 1996

October	Securicor Recruitment Services acquires Round Peg Recruitment.	**1996**
December	Securicor Communications acquires a majority stake in an American company, Intek Diversified Corporation, a private mobile radio specialist.	
February	Securicor Custodial Services enters US corrections market through Securicor New Century Inc, based in Virginia.	**1997**
April	Securicor Fuelserv acquires Thistle Fuels and Scots Fuels.	
	An internal reorganisation is implemented to ensure the quality of management succession. Within this exercise, Pony Express becomes Omega Same Day and the vehicle management companies are transferred to the Distribution division. Recruitment Services is transferred to the Security division and Business Services ceases to exist as a division.	
May	Securicor Omega Logistics acquires John Miller Transport.	
July	Securicor Telesciences, renamed Axiom Inc, undergoes a partial flotation on the US NASDAQ stock exchange.	
August	Ed Hough leaves the Group.	
September	Securicor 3net is sold.	
	The subscriber bases of Securicor Cellular Services are sold.	

Index

Acknowledgements

The story of Securicor could not have been written without generous help from a number of individuals, many of whom you will meet while turning the pages of this book. Others who deserve particular thanks are: Major Robert Peat, who chronicled the early life of the company and, sadly, died before this book was written; Denis Norton, the inspiration behind this publication and a great help at every step along the way; Peter Corner, who willingly made available his archive of both text and pictures; and Rachel Taylor, the financial expert whose contribution to the performance chapter of the book was invaluable.

It should not be forgotten that it is the people who dedicated their careers to Securicor in the past and the many thousands who work within the Group today who have made this story come to life. Thanks are due to each and every one of them.